MALAGA TRAVEL GUIDE 2024

Your Essential Companion to the Sun-Drenched Splendor of Malaga to Navigate Hidden Gems, Savor Local Flavors, Live Like a Local And Experience Adventures Beyond the Beaches.

NICHOLAS INGRAM

I

Malaga, situated in the Province of Malaga, serves as a significant municipality within Andalusia, Spain. Ranking as the second most populous city in Andalucía and the sixth in Spain overall, it occupies a prominent position in Southern Iberia along the renowned Costa del Sol (Coast of the Sun). Notably, Malaga proudly claims itself as the birthplace of the esteemed artist Pablo Picasso. Renowned for its vibrant history, delectable Mediterranean cuisine, locally produced wines, and inviting sandy beaches, Malaga encapsulates the essence of a captivating destination. Having transitioned from a city steeped in Moorish heritage to one celebrated for its culinary delights and lively festivities, Malaga stands out as an extraordinary locale to explore and savor.

The sun-soaked city of Malaga murmurs untold tales carried by the gentle Mediterranean breeze. Envision cobblestone streets, resonating with the footfalls of Phoenician traders, Roman emperors, and Moorish sultans. Picture ancient fortresses perched on rocky cliffs, overlooking azure waters where Picasso once found inspiration. Malaga is a lively tapestry woven with threads of history, art, and nature, ready to be explored. Close your eyes and feel the Andalusian sun's warm embrace as you meander through El Palmeral, a lush oasis where echoes of Moorish whispers linger among swaying palm trees. Imagine the enticing scent of freshly baked churros mingling with the fragrance of citrus groves, their golden fruits gleaming like jewels in the sunlight. Explore the grandeur of the Alcazaba, its ochre walls recounting stories of triumphs and defeats, of sultans and their courtly affairs. Ascend the winding Gibralfaro, letting the sea breeze carry the tang of salt as you survey the city below, a mosaic of terracotta rooftops and whitewashed buildings.

Enter the Picasso Museum, where the maestro's brilliance bursts forth in a riot of colors and shapes. Marvel at Roman amphitheaters where gladiators once clashed, their echoes reverberating in the heart of the contemporary city. Delight in tapas excursions, each bite a symphony of flavors, accompanied by the joyful strumming of flamenco guitars. As the twilight sky ignites in fiery hues, find yourself on La Malagueta beach, the sand beneath your feet warm, and the rhythmic roar of the ocean casting a hypnotic spell.

Malaga transcends being just a location; it's an immersive experience. It's the taste of gazpacho on a scorching afternoon, the clink of glasses filled with chilled red wine, and the laughter of locals resonating in squares adorned with orange blossoms. It's the excitement of uncovering hidden courtyards bursting with bougainvillea, the tranquility of ancient monasteries nestled in rolling hills, and the adrenaline rush of parasailing over the turquoise waters.

Are you prepared to unlock Malaga's hidden treasures? To immerse yourself in its rich history, savor its dynamic culture, and revel in its natural splendor? Come, dear traveler, and let Malaga enchant you with its magic. Your adventure awaits.

DISLCAIMER & COPYRIGHT NOTE

The information in this guide is based on the author's experiences, research, and knowledge up to the publication date. While efforts have been made to ensure accuracy, the author and publisher are not liable for changes, inaccuracies, or omissions after this date. Travel conditions may change, and readers should independently verify details before making arrangements. The author and publisher do not assume responsibility for readers' actions following the guide, as travel involves inherent risks. Readers are advised to exercise caution and make informed decisions based on their individual circumstances. | This travel guide is protected by copyright law. Reproduction, distribution, or transmission in any form without the author's prior written permission is prohibited, except for brief quotations in critical reviews and certain noncommercial uses allowed by copyright law. Unauthorized reproduction or distribution may result in civil and criminal penalties, including fines and imprisonment. Readers have a limited license for personal, non-commercial use; any other use requires explicit written permission. By accessing and using this guide, readers agree to respect the outlined copyright and disclaimer provisions. For permissions requests or complaints, please contact: *theworldexplorergs@gmail.com* | Copyright © 2024 **Nicholas Ingram**

Cover Image: Antequera (A Town on the Costa del Sol Malaga) at sunset | **Image Creator & Copyright Owner:** Víctor Gómez - *http://machbel.com* | **License:** *https://creativecommons.org/licenses/by-nc-nd/2.0/* | **Notice:** Please be aware that the paperback version of this travel guide is printed in black and white on white paper. This includes any colored photos that may appear in the online version. Thank you for your understanding.

CONTENTS

INTRODUCTION: WELCOME TO MALAGA	1
Why choose Malaga for Your Vacation?	3
History	5
Geography	6
Economy	7
Travel Tips	8
Maps	9
CHAPTER 1: GETTING STARTED	10
Best Times to Visit	11
Getting to Malaga from Different Parts of the World	12
Budgeting for Your Malaga Travel	13
Planning a Trip to Malaga on a Budget	15
Visas	17
Travel Insurance	19
CHAPTER 2: NAVIGATING	21
Getting around	22
Top 15 Neighborhoods of Malaga to Explore	24
CHAPTER 3: EXPLORING MALAGA	27
25 Must-Visit Attractions	28
Top 10 Beautiful Beaches	42
Sightseeing & Landmarks	45
Malaga Parks & Gardens	46
Cruising Malaga	49
Top 10 Must-Visit Museums	50
15 Malaga City Hidden Gems	55

Secret Courtyards and Charming Plazas	63
CHAPTER 4: SAVORING THE LOCAL FLAVORS	65
Food in Malaga	66
25 Must-try Local Dishes	67
Top Breakfast Restaurants	73
Top Brunch Spots	74
Top Lunch Spots	75
Top 20 Tapas You Must Try	76
Top 5 Tapas Spots	80
Authentic Seafood Joints	82
Top Bar To Have a Drink Like a Local	84
6 Best Places to Enjoy Wine	85
The Best Food Markets	86
Top 5 Malaga Cuisine Cooking Classes	88
10 Hidden Gem Restaurants	90
CHAPTER 5: VIBRANT FESTIVALS & CULTURAL EVENTS	95
Street Festivals in Málaga	96
Cultural Events in Málaga	98
Music Festivals in & Around Málaga	99
Malaga Annual Events Calendar	101
CHAPTER 6: ACCOMMODATION: 25 BEST PLACES	103
Best Luxury Hotels in Malaga	104
Mid-Range Accommodation in Malaga	105
Best Budget Friendly Accommodation in Malaga	107
Family-Friendly Places to Stay in Malaga	108
Best Boutique Hotels	109
Best Beach Resorts Near Malaga	110
CHAPTER 7: TOP 10 OUTDOOR ACTIVITIES TO ENJOY IN	111

MALAGA

CHAPTER 8: SHOPPING & SOUVENIRS	113
Sourvenir to Buy	115
Top 15 Things to Buy as Souvenir	116
Top 8 Shopping Area	118
Top 10 Shopping Centres & Malls	120
Top Tips for Souvenir Shopping	122
CHAPTER 9: NIGHTLIFE & ENTERTAINMENT	123
Top Neighborhoods for Partying in Málaga	125
The Best Night Clubs in Málaga	126
The Finest Night Bars in Málaga	128
Best Rooftop Bars in Málaga	129
Theaters, Cinemas, & Other Entertainment Options	130
CHAPTER 10: 11 UNFORGETTABLE DAY EXCURSIONS FROM MALAGA	131
Marbella	133
Ronda	136
Nerja & The Caves	140
Caminito del Rey	145
Gibraltar	148
Fuengirola	152
Cordoba	154
Seville	158
Granada	162
Mijas Pueblo	167
Antequera	171
Resources for Day Trips from Malaga	175
CHAPTER 11: PRACTICAL INFORMATION & TIPS	176

Staying Safe in Malaga	177
Emergency Contact Information	178
Staying Healthy in Malaga	179
18 Essential Apps For Visiting Malaga	180
Tourist Information Centers	183
Sustainable Travel	184
7 Ways to Make Your Malagan Trips More Eco-friendly	185
55 USEFUL Spanish Language Phrases	186
Map of Malaga with Key Points of Interest	189
3-Day Malaga Adentures Itinerary	190
CONCLUSION	192
BONUS: 43 Exciting Activities to Enjoy in Malaga	193
Other Books By This Author	195
About The Author	199

INTRODUCTION: WELCOME TO MALAGA

Envision a city nestled against the sapphire Mediterranean, where Phoenician traders exchanged secrets over spices, Roman legions paraded beneath triumphant arches, and Moorish sultans crafted intricate tales in silk and stone. This is Malaga, a lively port where history resonates from ancient ramparts, reverberates in concealed alleyways, and erupts onto vibrant canvases. But brace yourself, dear traveler, as our journey goes beyond sun-soaked beaches and tapas excursions. We are about to embark on a voyage through time, unraveling a pivotal event that forever left its imprint on Malaga's essence.

Transport yourself to the year 1487. The air is charged with tension as Christian forces, led by Ferdinand and Isabella, besiege Malaga—the last significant Muslim stronghold in Spain. For nearly three months, cannons thunder, catapults hurl fiery stones, and valiant warriors engage in a desperate struggle for supremacy. Eventually, after a grueling siege, the city walls crumble, and Malaga capitulates. However, this is more than a tale of victory and defeat; it marks a turning point, a pivotal moment in history.
Within the conquered city, cultures collide. Mosques transform into churches, Arabic whispers intertwine with Latin prayers, and a new era unfolds. Yet, Malaga's essence endures, simmering beneath the surface like the city's iconic gazpacho. Here is where our narrative takes a captivating turn. As Christians seek to erase the past, a clandestine resistance emerges.

Crypto-Muslims, covertly adhering to their faith, establish an underground network, preserving traditions and resisting assimilation.

Now, accompany me into the shadows. Traverse secret chambers adorned with faded Quranic verses, decode messages hidden in everyday objects, and witness the tenacity of a culture unwilling to be extinguished. This is the core of Malaga, a city where past and present coexist, secrets linger beneath the surface, and every cobblestone murmurs stories of resilience and cultural fusion.

But our journey doesn't conclude there. This defining event not only shaped Malaga's soul but also laid the groundwork for its artistic renaissance. Centuries later, a young Pablo Picasso, born amidst the echoes of this tumultuous past, would channel his city's vibrant spirit into groundbreaking art, forever altering the world's cultural landscape.

So, are you prepared to delve into the depths of Malaga's history, where pirates sailed the seas, emperors etched their legacies in stone, and resilient cultures defied extinction? This "Travel Guide to Malaga" transcends a mere map and list of sights; it is a key unlocking a city's hidden soul, a passport to a vibrant past that continues to shape its present, promising to ignite your imagination. Pack your bags, dear traveler, and let Malaga cast its enchantment upon you.

WHY CHOOSE MALAGA FOR YOUR VACATION?

There are numerous compelling reasons to contemplate a visit to Malaga. Here are just a few:

1. Breathtaking Beaches And Sunny Climate: Malaga boasts over 15 kilometers of coastline, providing a diverse range of beaches. Whether you seek lively urban beaches with water sports or tranquil coves for relaxation, the city's warm Mediterranean climate, characterized by mild winters and hot, sunny summers, makes it an ideal year-round beach destination.

2. Abundant History and Culture: Malaga's rich history, dating back to the Phoenicians, Romans, and Moors, is evident throughout the city. Explore the remarkable Alcazaba fortress, meander through the charming old town, and marvel at the Roman Theatre. With over 30 museums, including the Picasso Museum featuring a collection of the renowned artist's early works, Malaga is a cultural treasure trove.

3. Vibrant Art Scene: Malaga is a haven for art enthusiasts, boasting a thriving contemporary art scene and numerous galleries showcasing local and international artists. As the birthplace of Pablo Picasso, the city offers opportunities to delve into his life and work at the Picasso Museum and the Fundación Picasso Museo Casa Natal.

4. Delectable Cuisine and Wine: A paradise for food lovers, Malaga offers fresh seafood, tapas bars, and traditional Andalusian dishes. Local specialties like gazpacho, salmorejo, and pescaíto frito are must-try delights. The city also features a burgeoning wine scene, with several vineyards in the surrounding region.

5. Lively Nightlife: Malaga comes to life after dark, offering a diverse array of bars, clubs, and flamenco tablaos. Whether you crave a vibrant pub crawl or a traditional flamenco performance, the city has something for every nocturnal adventurer.

6. Strategic Base for Andalusian Exploration: Malaga's ideal location facilitates exploration of the rest of Andalusia, a region steeped in history, culture, and natural beauty. Day trips to cities like Granada, Seville, and Córdoba, or visits to the Sierra Nevada mountains or the thrilling Caminito del Rey hike with breathtaking views, are easily accessible.

7. Affordable Travel: Malaga proves to be a relatively budget-friendly destination, particularly when compared to other major European cities. With favorable deals on flights, accommodation, and activities, it offers excellent value for a memorable vacation.

HISTORY

Malaga's history is a tapestry woven with the threads of diverse civilizations, shaping its identity as a vibrant city on the Costa del Sol in southern Spain. Its origins trace back to prehistoric times, with evidence of settlements dating to the Bronze Age. The Phoenicians established the city's first known settlement around 770 BC, naming it 'Malaka'. This trading post flourished under subsequent Greek rule in the 6th century BC. In the 3rd century BC, Malaga fell under Carthaginian control before being annexed by the Romans in the 2nd century BC. Roman influence left an indelible mark on the city, evident in its infrastructure and status as a vital port and commercial hub. The Visigoths and then the Moors, who arrived in the 8th century AD, successively ruled Malaga. The Moorish era saw the city thrive culturally and architecturally, with iconic landmarks like the Alcazaba Fortress and Gibralfaro Castle erected. In 1487, Catholic Monarchs Ferdinand and Isabella claimed Malaga during the Reconquista, marking a turbulent period marked by the Inquisition and subsequent decline. The 19th and 20th centuries heralded Malaga's revival, fueled by industries like textiles and agriculture. Its transformation into a sought-after tourist destination, blessed with sunny beaches and a rich cultural heritage, further propelled its resurgence.

Today, Malaga stands as a bustling metropolis steeped in history and alive with cultural vibrancy. Its historic center beckons visitors with landmarks like the Alcazaba, Gibralfaro Castle, and the Picasso Museum, embodying the city's enduring allure and captivating charm.

GEOGRAPHY

Malaga, a coastal gem in southern Spain within the Andalusia region, rests gracefully along the Mediterranean shore. Bordered by the Axarquía mountains to the north and the Guadalhorce River valley to the west, the city center nestles near the confluence of the Guadalhorce and Guadalmedina rivers, with the Totalán Creek marking its eastern boundary. **_Geographically_**, Malaga boasts a diverse landscape, from mountainous terrain to sandy beaches, interwoven with urban and rural expanses. The Montes de Malaga mountain range provides a picturesque backdrop, with Pico Reina soaring to 1,031 meters (3,383 feet) above sea level. Along the coastline, sandy beaches stretch out amidst cliffs and rocky coves, defining Malaga's scenic shoreline. **_Malaga enjoys a subtropical Mediterranean climate_**, characterized by mild winters and hot summers. Average temperatures hover around 18°C (64°F) year-round, with peak summer temperatures reaching up to 30°C (86°F) in July and August. Conversely, January sees cooler temperatures around 12°C (54°F). Abundant sunshine graces Malaga for over 300 days annually, punctuated by occasional winter rainfall that sustains the verdant countryside. The city's coastal location moderates summer heat, offering a comfortable environment for outdoor pursuits such as sunbathing, swimming, and hiking. Sea temperatures remain inviting throughout the year, ranging from around 18°C in winter to 25°C in summer. **_With a population_** of 578,460 in the city (2020) and 1,700,752 in the province (2021), Malaga's demographic landscape has evolved, fueled by a significant influx of foreign nationals, surpassing 50,000 by 2020. This multicultural blend adds vibrancy to the city's dynamic atmosphere, enhancing its allure as a cherished destination for residents and tourists alike.

ECONOMY

Malaga's economy thrives on a diverse range of industries, with tourism leading the charge as the primary contributor. Millions of visitors flock to the region annually to bask in its rich culture, historical landmarks, and picturesque beaches, bolstering the province's GDP and providing ample employment opportunities. ***Ranked as the fourth-largest contributor to Spain's economy***, Malaga city stands alongside major urban centers like Madrid, Barcelona, and Valencia in driving economic growth. The agricultural sector plays a pivotal role, with Malaga's fertile lands yielding a bounty of avocados, oranges, lemons, mangoes, olive oil, and wine, which are not only vital for local consumption but also find their way onto international markets. Fishing adds further momentum to Malaga's economy, capitalizing on the region's abundant marine resources to supply a variety of fish species to local and global markets. In addition to these pillars, manufacturing, construction, and services such as education, healthcare, and retail contribute significantly to Malaga's economic landscape. The emergence of the technology and innovation sector, evidenced by the presence of startups, incubators, and multinational corporations like Google, Vodafone, Fujitsu Spain, and Oracle Corporation, underscores the city's commitment to diversifying its economy. Malaga's ***"Málaga: Open for Business"*** campaign has attracted foreign investments, further bolstering its economic prowess. The establishment of the Technological Park of Andalusia has provided a fertile ground for IT industries and other ventures to thrive. With a robust foundation built on tourism, agriculture, and fishing, coupled with burgeoning opportunities in emerging sectors, Malaga's economy continues to evolve, ensuring a promising future for the region and its residents.

TRAVEL TIPS

While Malaga is generally considered safe, it's still essential to take precautions to safeguard yourself during your visit. Here are some useful tips to help you stay safe while you visit Malaga:

1. Stay Vigilant: Pay attention to your surroundings, especially in busy areas, and remain alert for any suspicious behavior or individuals.

2. Secure Your Belongings: Keep your valuables like cash, credit cards, and passports secure and avoid carrying large sums of money or expensive items.

3. Use Reliable Transportation: Opt for licensed taxis, official tour companies, or public transport rather than unregulated services, which may pose risks.

4. Exercise Caution at Night: Avoid walking alone after dark, particularly in poorly lit or unfamiliar areas.

5. Beware of Pickpockets: Stay vigilant in crowded places like markets and public transport, where pickpocketing is common.

6. Respect Local Customs: Show respect for local customs and dress codes, especially when visiting religious or cultural sites.

7. Swim Safely: Take care when swimming in the sea or pools and adhere to safety guidelines.

8. Stay Hydrated: Given Malaga's hot climate, ensure you drink plenty of water and limit alcohol intake to stay hydrated.

By adhering to these safety measures, you can enhance your security and enjoy your time in Malaga with peace of mind.

MAPS

Scan This QR Code To Explore The Map Of Malaga

Scan This QR Code For A Printable Tourist Map Of Malaga

CHAPTER 1: GETTING STARTED

This chapter encompasses essential aspects of planning your trip to Malaga to ensure a seamless and budget-friendly travel experience. It begins by highlighting the best times to visit, considering weather, festivals, and local events emphasizing the charm of spring and fall, and unravel the nuances of Malaga's Mediterranean climate.

Exploring transportation options, the guide provides practical details on reaching Malaga from different parts of the world, offering transportation insights tailored to travelers from the United States, major European countries, and even Australia and New Zealand. A pivotal section focuses on budgeting, offering a comprehensive breakdown to help you plan your expenses efficiently. Gain valuable insights into Malaga's cost of living, sample budgets, and tips for maximizing your travel budget. This chapter also addresses visa requirements, providing clarity on entry procedures, and emphasizes the significance of obtaining comprehensive travel insurance for a worry-free exploration of this vibrant Spanish city.

Embark on a local's journey through Malaga with this insightful chapter, providing essential guidance for an authentic experience.

BEST TIMES TO VISIT

Malaga stands out as a favored spot for vacation, partly because of its Mediterranean climate. Best periods for a visit typically revolve around spring (April to June) and fall (September to October), characterized by agreeable weather and less overwhelming crowds. Here's a breakdown of the seasons:

1. Spring (April to June): Regarded as one of the prime times to explore Malaga, spring features mild and pleasant weather, with temperatures ranging between 15°C to 25°C (59°F to 77°F). The city comes alive with blooming flowers, enhancing its vibrancy.

2. Fall (September to October): Resembling spring, the fall season presents comfortable temperatures ranging from 18°C to 28°C (64°F to 82°F). As the summer crowds disperse, visitors can still relish warm weather and partake in cultural events.

3. Summer (July to August): Summer marks the peak tourist season, characterized by hot temperatures, often surpassing 30°C (86°F) & occasionally reaching up to 40°C (104°F). While beaches are popular, anticipate larger crowds & elevated prices during this period.

4. Winter (November to March): Malaga experiences mild winters compared to numerous European destinations, with daytime temperatures typically ranging from 10°C to 20°C (50°F to 68°F). Though less crowded, some attractions and beach activities may be less appealing due to cooler temperatures.

It's important to note that specific events, festivals, and local holidays could impact your choice of travel dates. Spring and fall strike a favorable balance between pleasant weather and fewer crowds, ensuring you have a more enjoyable experience in Malaga.

GETTING TO MALAGA FROM DIFFERENT PARTS OF THE WORLD

Regardless of your starting point, reaching Malaga is convenient thanks to the accessibility of **_Malaga-Costa del Sol Airport (AGP)._**

FROM THE UNITED STATES: **_Major airlines:_** Numerous carriers provide direct flights from major US cities such as New York, Chicago, Miami, Atlanta, and Boston. Well-known choices include American Airlines, Iberia, United Airlines, and Delta Air Lines. Flight durations typically range between 7-11 hours. **_Connecting flights:_** If direct flights are unavailable, convenient connecting options through European hubs like Madrid, Barcelona, or London are accessible.

FROM MAJOR EUROPEAN COUNTRIES: **_Direct flights:_** Several European airlines offer direct flights to Malaga from key cities like London, Paris, Amsterdam, Frankfurt, Munich, and Brussels. Flight durations are generally shorter, spanning 2-4 hours. **_Train travel:_** For a more scenic & environmentally friendly alternative, consider train travel within Europe. The Spanish high-speed AVE trains connect Malaga to cities as Madrid, Barcelona, and Seville in just a few hours.

FROM AUSTRALIA AND NEW ZEALAND: **_Long-haul flights:_** Due to the considerable distance, direct flights from Australia or New Zealand to Malaga are not available. Anticipate layovers in Asia or the Middle East, resulting in a total travel time of 20-30 hours. **_Multi-city flights:_** Consider breaking up your journey by including a stopover in another enticing destination like Dubai, Singapore, or Bangkok.

BUDGETING FOR YOUR MALAGA TRAVEL

Creating a budget for your Malaga trip is a smart way to ensure an enjoyable experience without exceeding your financial limits. Consider the following factors:

ACCOMMODATION

Accommodation Types: Malaga provides various options, ranging from budget-friendly hostels to luxurious hotels. Your choice significantly influences your budget, with hostels being the most economical and luxury hotels representing a higher cost. | **Location:** Accommodations in the city center tend to be pricier, but staying there can save on transportation expenses as most attractions are within walking distance. | **Time of Year:** Prices peak during July and August. Opting for the shoulder season (April-June and September-October) offers potential savings.

FOOD

Dining Out: Restaurants in tourist areas can be costly, but tapas bars provide affordable options. Cooking in your accommodation's kitchen is another budget-friendly alternative. | **Groceries:** Malaga's supermarkets offer reasonably priced groceries for those looking to prepare their own meals. | **Drinks:** Drinks, especially alcoholic ones, can be expensive. Consider buying from supermarkets rather than bars to save money.

ACTIVITIES

Free Activities: Explore the city center, stroll along the beach, and take advantage of free admission to the Picasso Museum on the first Sunday of each month. **Paid Activities:** Plan for expenses related to visiting attractions like the Alcazaba, Gibralfaro Castle, and the Malaga Cathedral.

TRANSPORTATION

Public Transportation: The Malaga City Card provides unlimited public transportation for a set duration, offering an efficient and cost-effective option. | **Walking:** Given Malaga's relatively small size, walking is a budget-friendly way to explore the city center at your own pace.

OTHER EXPENSES

Travel Insurance: Essential for medical coverage, lost luggage, and trip cancellation. | **Souvenirs:** Budget for souvenirs based on your preferences, ranging from a few euros to more substantial amounts.

SAMPLE BUDGET FOR A 5-DAY TRIP TO MALAGA (FOR ONE ERSON)

- Accommodation: €50 per night x 5 nights = €250
- Food: €20 per day x 5 days = €100
- Activities: €50 per day x 5 days = €250
- Transportation: €10 per day x 5 days = €50
- Other expenses: €50
- Total: €700

These figures are indicative, and your actual expenses may vary. Additional tips for saving money in Malaga include traveling during the shoulder season, booking accommodations and flights in advance, taking advantage of free activities, cooking your own meals, buying alcohol from supermarkets, utilizing public transportation or walking, avoiding tourist traps, and seeking tips from locals.

PLANNING A TRIP TO MALAGA ON A BUDGET

If you're considering a trip to Malaga and want to manage your expenses efficiently, here's a breakdown to help you budget for your journey:

Average Daily Cost: The typical daily expenditure for a traveler in Malaga is approximately $151 (€140). This includes various expenses like meals, local transportation, accommodation, and entertainment.

One Week Trip: For an individual, a one-week trip to Malaga is estimated to cost around $1,055 (€979). For a couple traveling together, the cost for a week increases to $2,111 (€1,958).

Two Weeks Trip: If you plan to stay for two weeks, the average cost for an individual is around $2,111 (€1,958). For a couple traveling together for two weeks, the estimated cost is $4,222 (€3,917).

One Month Trip: A one-month stay in Malaga is budgeted at approximately $4,523 (€4,197) for an individual. For a couple on a month-long trip, the estimated cost rises to $9,047 (€8,393).

Note: Prices may vary based on your travel style, speed, and other factors.

BREAKDOWN OF DAILY COSTS

1. Accommodation: The average cost for one person in a hotel or hostel is $80 (€75), while a double-occupancy room is around $161 (€149). *Hotel Price Range:* $65 - $171.

2. Local Transportation: Expect to spend $33 (€31) per day on taxis, local buses, or subway. *Recommended:* Consider services like Vip Transfer or airport transfers for convenience.

3. Food: The average daily cost for meals is $37 (€35). Breakfast is usually more affordable than lunch or dinner. Explore local dishes such as *Gazpachuelo Malagueno* and *Fritura Malaguena*.

4. Entertainment: Budget around $33 (€31) per day for entrance tickets, shows, and other activities. *Recommended:* Explore historical Segway tours or small-group tours with lunch.

5. Tips and Handouts: Allocate around $13 (€12) per day for tips or service providers.

6. Alcohol: Plan for an average daily expense of $24 (€22) on alcoholic beverages.

7. Water: On average, people spend $1.26 (€1.17) per day on bottled water.

Is Malaga Expensive? Malaga's prices are reasonable and comparable to other travel destinations. It is considered moderately priced within Europe, offering fair costs for accommodation, food, and sightseeing.

FINAL TIPS

Consider traveling independently for more affordability, freedom, and flexibility and Take advantage of local transportation options, such as buses and trains, for a more budget-friendly experience.

By utilizing this budget breakdown, you can plan your trip to Malaga with a clear understanding of potential expenses and make the most of your travel experience within your preferred budget constraints.

VISAS

If you are a citizen of a European Union (EU) or European Economic Area (EEA) country, you are not required to obtain a visa for travel to Spain. Citizens of these countries benefit from the right to free movement within the Schengen Area, which encompasses Spain. They can enter Spain for short stays, whether for tourism, business, or other purposes, using a valid passport or national identity card. However, citizens from ***non-EU or non-EEA countries*** may be subject to visa requirements depending on their nationality. Spain, being a Schengen Area member, has specific visa requirements applicable to citizens of certain countries.

Schengen Visa: The Schengen visa is a travel document that permits entry and travel within the Schengen Area. This region comprises 27 European countries that have agreed to eliminate passport control at their shared borders. It includes most EU member states and some non-EU nations like Norway, Switzerland, Iceland, and Liechtenstein. The Schengen visa allows travelers to visit one or more Schengen countries for a specified period, usually up to 90 days within a 180-day period. The visa caters to various purposes, including tourism, business, family visits, or medical treatment.

Application Process: To obtain a Schengen visa, individuals typically apply at the consulate or embassy of the main destination country in your travel itinerary. The application process involves submitting required documentation such as a valid passport, proof of travel insurance, evidence of accommodation, financial means to cover the trip, and a completed visa application form. Once processed and approved, a Schengen visa sticker is affixed to the passport, allowing you entry and travel within the Schengen Area. It's important to note that having a Schengen visa does not guarantee entry, as travelers may still undergo border checks upon arrival.

National Visa: For stays exceeding 90 days or for specific purposes like work, study, or family reunification, a National Visa, also known as a long-stay or type D visa, may be required. This visa allows an extended stay in Spain and often involves additional documentation tailored to the purpose of the visit. The application for a National Visa is typically submitted at the Spanish consulate or embassy in your home country or current residence.

Visa Exemptions: Certain countries, including EU and EEA nations, may be exempt from obtaining a visa for short stays in Spain. However, even if visa-exempt, travelers must still adhere to entry requirements, such as possessing a valid passport, adequate funds, and proof of onward travel.

Additional Requirements: Apart from a visa, you might be obligated to furnish additional documentation upon entry, such as travel insurance, accommodation reservations, or proof of sufficient funds. It is crucial to verify specific requirements based on your nationality and the purpose of your visit.

COVID-19 Travel Requirements: It is possible that Spain still has some specific entry requirements or restrictions related to COVID-19, including testing, quarantine, or vaccination prerequisites. It is advisable to check the latest information from Spanish authorities or the nearest Spanish consulate or embassy to you before planning your travel to Malaga.

TRAVEL INSURANCE

Spain ranks as the second-most visited country globally. It mandates all international travelers, including US citizens, planning visits from December 2023 onward, to obtain Spain travel insurance with a coverage minimum of €30,000 (approximately $50,000 USD), even for short stays. Proof of travel insurance for Spain may be requested by Spanish officials at the port of entry, emphasizing the importance of having adequate coverage for a seamless visit.

With its beloved cities, breathtaking landscapes, rich culture, lively villages hosting captivating festivals, and delectable cuisine, Spain attracts millions of tourists annually. The presence of over 1.5 million US citizens currently residing in Spain reflects the frequent travel of US citizens to Spain for various purposes, such as vacations, work, and visiting friends and family residing in the country. Madrid and Barcelona are the primary locations where a significant number of US citizens choose to live in Spain.

Embarking on a journey to Spain for leisure or to reunite with loved ones is an exhilarating experience. However, you should be mindful that international travel can be exhausting and may entail unforeseen risks. To address such uncertainties, you should get an insurance coverage for sudden travel and medical emergencies during your trip. This coverage encompasses expenses related to Trip Cancellation or Trip Delay, providing financial protection for the funds invested in the vacation.

Below are some recommended travel insurance companies for your Malaga/Spain travel:

1. TIN LEG: *Website:* https://www.tinleg.com | **Recommended Plan:** Gold | **Cost:** $274 | **Coverage:** Medical & Evacuation Limits Per Person - $500,000 / $500,000

2. GENERALI GLOBAL ASSISTANCE: *Website:* https://us.generaliglobalassistance.com/solutions/buy-travel-insurance-trip-cruise-vacation | *Recommended Plan:* Standard | *Cost:* $307 |

Coverage: Medical & Evacuation Limits Per Person - $50,000 / $250,000

3. TRAWICK INTERNATIONAL: *Website*: *https://www.trawickinternational.com.* | **Recommended Plan:** Safe Travels Voyager | *Cost:* $231 | *Coverage*: Medical & Evacuation Limits Per Person - $250,000 / $1,000,000

4. AXA ASSISTANCE USA: *Website:* https://www.axatravelinsurance.com | *Recommended Plan:* Platinum | *Cost:* $236 | *Coverage:* Medical & Evacuation Limits Per Person - $250,000 / $1,000,000

5. TRAVEL INSURED INTERNATIONAL: *Website:* *https://www.travelinsured.com* | *Recommended Plan:* Worldwide Trip Protector | *Cost:* $492 | *Coverage:* Medical & Evacuation Limits Per Person - $100,000 / $1,000,000

These insurance plans offer various coverage including medical expenses, evacuation, trip cancellation, and more. The prices for these plans may vary, and it's advisable to visit their respective websites for detailed quotes tailored to individual trip details.

CHAPTER 2: NAVIGATING MALAGA LIKE A LOCAL

GETTING AROUND

Malaga offers various transportation options for visitors to navigate the city which includes:

1. Walking: Walking is a cost-free and flexible way to explore Malaga. Tourist information centers can provide suggested walking routes, and guided tours are available for a fee.

2. Bicycles: Renting a bike is a faster alternative to walking, allowing visitors to cover more ground. Bike rental companies offer various options, including trekking bikes, mountain bikes, road bikes, and even fold-away bicycles. Guided bike tours are also available.

3. eBikes and eScooters: Pedal-assisted eBikes and eScooters are available for rent. Regulations have been introduced to manage their use in the city, with *Lime and Dott* being the authorized providers.

4. Bike Taxis (Trixis): Bike Taxis, known as Trixis, provide a quick and weather-protected way to tour the city. Passengers sit in covered pod-like carriages towed by bicycles, offering an eco-friendly and guided experience.

5. Segway: Segway tours provide a modern and fun way to sightsee. Various routes are available, often including entrance to monuments & museums, with prices averaging around 30 euros per hour.

6. Horse and Carriage: Horse-drawn carriages offer a traditional and romantic mode of transportation, particularly suitable for city parks and the port. Carriage rides typically cost around 30 euros for a 45-minute trip.

7. Train: Malaga's local train services connect the city with nearby areas along the coast and inland. The Alhameda train station is the local terminal station, and services extend to Fuengirola and Alhaurin.

8. Metro: Malaga has a two-line metro system connecting the city center to the west and south-west, starting from Maria Zambrano RENFE train station.

9. Bus - Local: EMT operates an efficient local bus network connecting various city center locations. Single bus tickets cost 1.30 euros, with options for rechargeable multi-trip cards & monthly season tickets.

10. Bus - To Other Places: Malaga Bus Station facilitates travel to other destinations. The city also offers a hop-on-hop-off tourist bus providing a convenient way to explore key attractions.

11. Car Hire: Car rental options are available at the airport, train station, and city center, offering flexibility for exploring Malaga and its surroundings.

12. Car Parks and Street Parking: Underground car parks are available throughout the city, and street parking is limited. Pay-and-display systems apply to designated parking spaces.

13. Taxis: Taxis are widely available in Malaga, with numerous ranks throughout the city. The minimum taxi fare is 3.17 euros, and different fares apply based on the time and day of the week.

In addition, the hop-on-hop-off tourist bus provides a comprehensive way to discover Malaga, with both red and green routes covering major attractions. Tickets are valid for 24 hours, allowing visitors to explore at their own pace.

TOP 15 NEIGHBORHOODS OF MALAGA TO EXPLORE

Discovering the ideal neighborhood in Malaga is essential for a satisfying experience in this vibrant Spanish city. Home to over 600,000 people, Malaga offers diverse neighborhoods with unique atmospheres. Here's a breakdown of the top 15 neighborhoods to help you make an informed decision on which area to stay during your visit.

1. Centro Historico: The historical center boasts picturesque, pedestrianized streets filled with locals and tourists. It offers a cultural hub with attractions like the Picasso Museum and the Alcazaba fortress. | ***Best for:*** Proximity to major sites, vibrant atmosphere, excellent food and drink.

2. La Goleta: Located northwest of Centro Historico, La Goleta is undergoing gentrification. It caters to those seeking a central location without breaking the bank, featuring trendy bars and affordable dining options. | ***Best for:*** Affordability, connecting with young locals, central living on a budget.

3. Soho: Southwest of Centro Historico, Soho is a creative hub with street art, vintage stores, & independent businesses. It hosts the Contemporary Art Center & the monthly "Made in Soho" market. | ***Best for:*** Artistic vibes, mingling with hipsters, exploring businesses.

4. La Merced: Bordering Centro Historico to the northeast, La Merced is known for its lively nightlife & numerous bars & restaurants. The central square, *Plaza de la Merced*, is a popular hangout spot. **Best for:** Vibrant nightlife, bustling atmosphere, abundant dining options.

5. Laguinallas: East of La Merced, Laguinallas is a residential area with street art & a laid-back atmosphere. It's an affordable option close to the city center, making it suitable for those on a budget. | **Best for:** Living among locals, affordability, city center outskirts.

6. Plaza de Toros Vieja: Southeast of Soho, Plaza de Toros Vieja is a small, family-oriented district with a quiet ambiance. It offers riverside stretches and proximity to O2 Centro Wellness El Perchel. | **Best for:** Quiet living, family-focused, work-oriented.

7. Segalerva: In the far north, Segalerva is a domestic neighborhood close to La Rosaleda Stadium and Parque San Miguel. Ideal for families, it houses the Academia De Ingles Avenida International. | **Best for**: Far north of the center, good schools, quiet living.

8. La Malagueta: East of the city center, it is renowned for its extensive beach, shopping centers, & cultural venues like Center Pompidou. It's a sought-after area but comes with a higher price tag. | **Best for:** Beach living, proximity to cultural venues, shopping.

9. El Palo: Located around 4 miles east of Centro Historico, El Palo offers a quiet life among locals with beautiful beaches, traditional boats, and a mix of modern and traditional charm. | **Best for:** Local experience, quality of life, peaceful living.

10. El Limonar: El Limonar is an affluent residential district situated to the east of the city center. Recognized for its elegant villas, tree-lined avenues, and breathtaking views of the Mediterranean Sea, this locality appeals to families and individuals seeking a serene lifestyle while maintaining proximity to urban conveniences. El Limonar is also home to some of the top schools in Malaga, making it an optimal choice for families with school-aged children.

11. Pedregalejo: Pedregalejo is a charming coastal neighborhood characterized by its relaxed ambiance. Popular among both locals and expatriates, it is renowned for its picturesque beaches, seafood eateries, and traditional fishermen's dwellings. Ideal for those desiring a laid-back life by the sea yet still within reach of the city center, Pedregalejo's beachside promenade provides a perfect setting for leisurely evening walks and enjoying the sunset.

12. Teatinos: Teatinos is a contemporary residential area positioned to the northwest of the city center. Attracting students and young professionals, it is home to the University of Malaga and various business parks. Offering diverse housing options, from budget-friendly apartments to luxurious villas, Teatinos boasts ample green spaces, sports facilities, and shopping centers, providing a convenient and comfortable living environment.

13. Huelin: Huelin is a traditional, working-class neighborhood located west of the city center, renowned for its vibrant atmosphere with numerous bars, restaurants, and shops. Home to the Automobile and Fashion Museum, it holds appeal for culture enthusiasts. Huelin provides affordable housing choices, making it an attractive option for first-time homebuyers and investors

14.Ciudad Jardin: meaning Garden City, is a sizable residential district positioned to the southwest of the city center. Noteworthy for its expansive green areas, parks, and sports facilities, it caters to families and outdoor enthusiasts. Ciudad Jardin offers a variety of housing options, ranging from apartments to townhouses and villas, accommodating diverse budgets and preferences.

15. Churriana: Churriana is a suburban neighborhood located to the south of the city center, near Malaga's airport. Recognized for its scenic countryside, traditional Andalusian residences, and tranquil atmosphere, Churriana is ideal for those seeking a peaceful lifestyle while still enjoying close proximity to urban amenities. This area is also favored by golf enthusiasts, as it hosts several golf courses.

CHAPTER 3: EXPLORING MALAGA

25 MUST-VISIT ATTRACTIONS

Malaga beckons with its rich tapestry of cultural and historical wonders, inviting you to explore its ancient marvels and modern delights. From the 13th-century Alcazaba fortress to magnificent Baroque cathedrals, the city's landmarks tell stories of centuries past. But Malaga offers more than just history; it's a vibrant blend of old and new. Wander its charming streets and discover restaurants serving kangaroo dishes alongside live flamenco performances. Delve into museums showcasing the revolutionary works of local painters, bridging the gap between tradition and innovation. And amidst it all, the city's stunning vistas of the Costa de Sol and its beautiful beaches, parks, and gardens offer moments of relaxation and enjoyment. With every step, Malaga captivates with its old-world charm and modern allure, promising countless opportunities for exploration and memorable experiences.

1. ALCAZABA DE MÁLAGA

The Alcazaba of Málaga, originally erected in the 11th century atop a former Roman bastion, stands as a testament to Moorish architectural prowess. Serving as a formidable stronghold for the Kingdom of Granada, this majestic fortress boasts over 100 towers and three formidable defensive walls. Perched atop the Monte de Gibralfaro, it is renowned as one of the most well-preserved Alcazabas in the region. A visit to the Alcazaba of Málaga is a must for history enthusiasts and sightseers alike, offering breathtaking panoramas of the city and the sparkling Mediterranean Sea. Explore its captivating gardens, picturesque courtyards, and evocative historical ruins to uncover the rich tapestry of its past. | **Address:** Calle Alcazabilla, 2, 29012, Malaga, Spain. | **Website:** *http://www.alcazabamalaga.com* | **Opening hours:** Summer (1 June to 30 Sep) : 9:00 to 20:00 daily | Winter (1 Oct to 31 May): 9:00 to 18:00 daily

Alcazaba de Málaga, Authored by Cayetano

2. MALAGA CATHEDRAL (CATEDRAL DE LA ENCARNACIÓN DE MÁLAGA)

The Malaga Cathedral, also affectionately known as La Manquita (the one-armed lady), stands as a stunning example of Renaissance architecture blended with elements of Gothic, Baroque, and Neoclassical styles. Conceived by Diego Siloe between the 16th and 18th centuries, the cathedral was built upon the site of a former mosque, symbolizing the transition from Muslim rule spanning eight centuries. Notably, the main façade and south tower remain unfinished, adding to its intriguing allure. Beyond its magnificent sculptures and antique architectural features, the cathedral also houses a museum, offering visitors a deeper insight into its rich history and significance. | **Address:** C. Molina Lario, 9, 29015, Malaga, Spain. | **Website:** www.Malagacatedral.com | **Opening hours**: Mon – Fri: 10:00 – 18:00, Sat: 10:00 – 17:00, Sun: Closed | Entrance is free on Sundays from 14:00 to 18:00 (only for Malagueños).

Málaga Cathedral - Catedral de Málaga, Imaged Authored by Trevor Huxham

3. GIBRALFARO CASTLE (CASTILLO DE GIBRALFARO)

Constructed in the 10th century under the Caliph of Cordoba's rule, this commanding hilltop castle underwent expansion in the 14th century by the Sultan of Granada. Strolling along its turrets offers panoramic views of the ocean and the surrounding landscape for miles. It's no surprise that the Catholic Monarchs Ferdinand and Isabella faced a formidable challenge in taking the castle from the Moors during the famous Siege of Málaga in 1487, requiring three months to succeed. Their victory was attributed to the besieged running out of food and water rather than a straightforward conquest. Similar to the Alcazaba, with which it was connected in the 14th century, the Gibralfaro is remarkably well-preserved and has undergone expert restoration where needed. This preservation allows visitors to grasp why it was once considered the most impregnable fortress in mainland Spain. Perched atop the slopes of Mount Gibralfaro, the remnants of Gibralfaro Castle command a majestic presence overlooking the cityscape and the azure expanse of the Mediterranean Sea. It was constructed upon the foundations of a Phoenician lighthouse, giving rise to its name derived from the Arabic and Greek term 'gebel-faro,' meaning 'rock of the lighthouse.' While time has weathered much of the castle, You can still marvel at the formidable old ramparts that endure as tangible relics of its storied past. | **Address**: Cam. Gibralfaro, 11, 29016 Malaga, Spain.

View of Castle of Gibralfaro from Malaga Palacio hotel - Image Authored by Danielmlg86

Malaga, Plaza de la Merced - Image Created By Banja & Frans Mulder

4. PLAZA DE LA MERCED

Plaza de la Merced, a bustling square in the heart of Malaga's La Merced neighborhood, serves as a vibrant hub for both locals and visitors alike. It's not only the birthplace of Pablo Picasso but also a modern-day hotspot teeming with bars, restaurants, and sun-soaked terraces, perfect for unwinding. Street performers add to the lively atmosphere, providing live entertainment as you enjoy traditional tapas. Beyond the square, the surrounding streets like Calle Alamo and Calle Carreteria beckon with trendy bars and clubs, making La Merced a hedonist's paradise. Amidst it all, Casa Natal de Picasso and the Monumento a Torrijos stand as reminders of the area's rich cultural heritage. Whether you're exploring the exhibitions or simply soaking in the ambiance, Plaza de la Merced promises an unforgettable experience in Malaga. | **Address:** Plaza de la Merced, 25, 29012 Malaga, Spain.

5. SEA LIFE BENALMÁDENA

Sea Life Benalmádena offers an immersive experience into the wonders of marine life, serving as both an aquarium and marine biology research center located in Benalmádena, a suburb of Malaga. Visitors can marvel at exotic marine creatures, including the largest seahorse collection in the Costa del Sol region, as well as encounter a 100-year-old turtle and awe-inspiring sharks in the Jurassic Tunnel. The aquarium provides interactive feeding sessions for sharks, otters, rays, and seahorses, allowing guests to engage firsthand with these fascinating creatures. | **Address:** Av. del Puerto Deportivo, s/n, 29630 Benalmádena, Malaga, Spain.

6. SANTA MARÍA DE LA VICTORIA

Basílica de Santa María de la Victoria, Málaga -
image Authored By David Jones

The Santa María de la Victoria Basilica, dating back to the early 16th century, began as a chapel before being reconstructed into a Baroque church around 1700. One of the main draws of this historic church is its pantheon and crypt, which are dedicated to the Counts of Buenavista. | **Address:** Plaza Santuario, s/n, 29012 Malaga, Spain.

7. THE HOLY MARTYRS CHURCH (IGLESIA DE LOS SANTOS MARTIRES)

The Holy Martyrs Church, also known as Iglesia De Los Santos Martires, was commissioned by the Catholic Monarchs following their conquest of Spain in 1487. Dedicated to the saints and martyrs Ciriaco and Paula, who were slain in Malaga for their unwavering faith, the church originally embodied a Gothic-Mudejar architectural style. Its interior underwent a Baroque transformation, resulting in an aesthetically pleasing blend of styles. The Mudejar tower remains a notable feature, standing proudly outside the church. | **Address:** Plaza de los Martires, 29008 Malaga, Spain.

8. ST. JAMES CHURCH (IGLESIA DE SANTIAGO APÓSTOL)

Founded in 1490, St. James Church, or Iglesia de Santiago Apóstol, holds the distinction of being Malaga's oldest church, constructed atop the grounds of a former mosque. The church boasts a predominantly Baroque-style interior, characterized by its stunning architectural details. Of particular significance is the presence of Pablo Picasso's baptismal certificate, marking his christening in 1881. The church features three naves adorned with notable works by artists such as Alonso Cano and Niño de Guevara. | **Address:** C. Granada, 78, 29015 Malaga, Spain.

9. CHURCH OF SAN JUAN BAUTISTA (IGLESIA DE SAN JUAN BAUTISTA)

The Church of San Juan Bautista, situated in Vélez-Málaga, was among the four churches established by the Catholic Monarchs following their conquest of the city in 1487. Dedicated to John the Baptist, this Roman Catholic church initially featured a Gothic Mudejar architectural style. Over the years, it underwent multiple renovations, with the last major overhaul occurring in 1860. | **Address:** Calle San Juan 3, 29005 Malaga, Spain.

10. ROMAN THEATRE MALAGA (TEATRO ROMANO DE MÁLAGA)

Teatro romano de Málaga - Image Authored by Jorge Castro Ruso

Málaga's Roman theatre, the oldest monument in the city and one of the few surviving Roman structures in Andalusia, holds a prominent place at the base of the Alcazaba. This area in the heart of Málaga is not only historically significant but also exceptionally beautiful, representing one of the noteworthy sites in southern Spain. Constructed in the 1st century AD, the theatre remained in use until the 3rd century AD before falling into neglect. In the 8th century, when the Moors settled in Málaga, they did not show much regard for this once-magnificent entertainment venue, using its materials to build the Alcazaba. In 1951, during the construction of an arts center, the theatre was rediscovered, leading to a complex and lengthy restoration process. It finally opened to the public in 2011 and now hosts concerts and plays, featuring an informative visitors' center. Comprising three distinct sections, the theatre features the stands (cavea), the orchestra pit, and the stage (proscenium), offering visitors a glimpse into ancient Roman architectural and cultural heritage. For more information, you can contact Teatro Romano at Calle Alcazabilla, S/N, Málaga, Spain, or call +34 951 50 11 15.

11. EL CHORRO

Walkway along a Steep Wall of a Gorge in El Chorro

El Chorro is a picturesque village nestled in the Malaga province amidst the stunning mountains of the Guadalhorce Natural Park. Renowned for its adventurous spirit, the village draws hundreds of thrill-seekers each year. It has earned a reputation as a climber's paradise, thanks to its exceptional rock formations. Visitors to El Chorro can rent bikes and immerse themselves in a day of exploration amid the breathtaking Andalusian scenery. Additionally, a visit to the famous Caminito Del Rey is a must-do experience. This 100-year-old mountain walkway, suspended 100 feet above sheer cliffs, offers an unforgettable adventure for those seeking an adrenaline rush.

12. EL PIMPI RESTAURANT

A visit to Málaga would be incomplete without experiencing El Pimpi, one of the city's oldest and most cherished dining establishments. Whether it's for a pre-lunch or early evening vermouth (red Martini over ice), the outdoor terrace provides a perfect setting with views of the Moorish Alcazaba and the Roman amphitheater, allowing you to observe the lively activity on Calle Alcazabilla. The attentive service from a team of waiters mirrors the hospitality of the original pimpis – friendly locals who assisted sailors unloading their goods at Málaga's port and guided them to places for drinks and snacks. Highly recommended at El Pimpi are the mini buey (ox) burgers and the homemade croquetas, adding to the culinary delight of the experience.

13. PICASSO MUSEUM

Following lunch or drinks at El Pimpi, consider heading next door to the impeccably preserved Picasso Museum to appreciate the artistic legacy of Málaga's most renowned native. Established in 2003 by Christine and Bernard Ruiz-Picasso, Picasso's daughter-in-law and grandson, the museum's permanent collection showcases over 200 works spanning every phase of Picasso's diverse career. Additionally, over the next three years, until March 2016, the museum will exhibit an additional 166 Picasso pieces, including some rarely seen by the public before.

Picasso Museum

14. MÁLAGA PORT

In recent years, the oldest continuously operated port in Spain has undergone a remarkable transformation, evolving into one of the most aesthetically pleasing and lively areas in Málaga. The addition of the 'Palm Garden of Surprises' along the promenade has contributed to the tropical ambiance of the surroundings. At the far end, near Málaga's historic bullring, stands the Pompidou Centre, Málaga's equivalent to the renowned Parisian gallery, distinguished by a large, multi-colored cube. Adjacent to it is the Paseo del Muelle Uno, a bustling thoroughfare lined with bars and restaurants that leads to the Malagueta beach. This area has become an ideal spot for an early evening stroll or to observe the impressive cruise liners as they embark on their voyages around the Mediterranean. Centre Pompidou Málaga can be found at Muelle Uno, Puerto de Málaga, Pasaje Doctor Carrillo Casaux, s/n, Muelle 1, Málaga. For further information, you can contact them at +34 951 92 62 00.

Malaga Port

15. BAR LA TRANCA

La Tranca primarily attracts locals from Málaga, offering an unparalleled opportunity to immerse yourself in the vibrant street life of La Merced. The small bar overflows onto Calle Carreteria, creating a bustling atmosphere where patrons are generously served vermouth, sweet wines, and homemade tapas by the lively owner, Ezequiel. The ambiance is characterized by noise and chaos, embodying the quintessential traits of a genuinely local bar in Andalusia. The back wall of Tranca is adorned with album covers featuring classic Spanish singers, spanning genres from pop to flamenco, creating a nostalgic backdrop. Despite its unassuming charm, La Tranca stands out as one of the best bars in Málaga that often goes undiscovered by tourists.

16. MERCADO DE LA MERCED

Exploring Málaga's prominent architectural attractions can be quite thirst-inducing, especially during the spring or summer months. Fortunately, the city center is teeming with options for dining and drinking. One of the trendiest spots to enjoy a cold beer and some tapas is Mercado de la Merced. After undergoing a six-month makeover, the market reopened in October 2015, emerging as one of the city's most stylish places for culinary delights and beverages. Boasting 22 stalls, Mercado de la Merced offers an array of offerings, including cured hams, fresh fish, vegetables, designer tapas bars, and sushi stalls. Positioned in the heart of the fashionable La Merced neighborhood, the market is conveniently just a five-minute walk from

Málaga's old town.

17. VINO MIO RESTAURANT

For a unique dining experience in Málaga, few places rival Vino Mio, located just a few minutes' walk from Plaza de la Merced, in terms of friendliness and originality. In fact, it might be the only restaurant in Andalusia where you can savor dishes like kangaroo and crocodile while enjoying a live Flamenco show. This creative blend of artistic and culinary pleasures transforms dining at Vino Mio into a highly enjoyable experience, complemented by the warm and efficient service from the waiting staff. At the end of the Flamenco show, the dancer invites diners to join and try their hand at flamenco, adding a memorable touch to an evening at this quirky restaurant.

18. MERCADO DEL CARMEN

If you're in the mood for a break from monuments and crave an authentic Málaga experience, make your way to El Perchel's Mercado del Carmen. Once inside, you'll encounter the typical hustle and bustle of bargaining and socializing, along with what many locals claim to be the finest fish and seafood stalls in town. El Carmen is situated in the historic neighborhood of 'El Perchel,' named after the hooks ('perchas') where local fishermen used to hang their daily catch to dry. Despite being surrounded by trendy tapas joints, this market has retained its genuinely local ambiance and the delightful, distinctly fishy aromas. You can savor the freshest catches as tapas in one of the numerous nearby bars.

19. MERCADO ATARAZANAS

The stunning Moorish entrance of the Atarazanas appears more fitting for Granada's Alhambra than as an adornment for an upscale supermarket. However, Málaga's grandest market has undergone numerous transformations. The archway is the sole remnant of the original 14th-century seven-arched structure, which served as a colossal shipyard during Málaga's Arabic rule when the sea extended further inland than today. Following the Catholic monarchs' conquest of Málaga from the Moors in 1487, the Atarazanas was repurposed as a convent. Over the centuries, the building has served various functions, including a military fort, a hospital, and a medical school. Don't miss the beautiful stained-glass window on its rear facade, depicting fishing boats navigating Málaga's bustling port.

20. BAR LOS GATOS

Los Gatos is among the most welcoming bars in Málaga, where first-time visitors are greeted as if they've been loyal patrons for two decades. The decor is traditional, featuring a large stuffed bull and bullfighting memorabilia in one corner, along with an assortment of trinkets and antique items scattered throughout the restaurant. Los Gatos successfully caters to both locals and visitors, extending warm welcomes in both English and Spanish. Its strategic location just off Calle Granada, the central street in the historical quarter, makes it an ideal spot to enjoy a cold beer and tapas while exploring the nearby monuments.

21. SOHO STREET ART

You won't find many tourists wandering the streets of Soho, a somewhat overlooked district in Málaga that, around fifty years ago, was considered a desirable residential area. Enclosed by Alameda Principal to the north, the Guadalmedina river to the west, and the port to the east, this currently neglected neighborhood is, nevertheless, home to one of the most dynamic and innovative street art scenes in Andalusia. Under the initiative called Málaga Arte Urbano Soho (MAUS), some of the world's leading graffiti artists have adorned Soho's crumbling facades with incredible spray-paint images.

Exploring these artworks is an excellent way to spend a morning or afternoon away from the typical tourist circuit, and the best part is that it's entirely free.

22. LA MALAGUETA BEACH

This man-made stretch of fine sand, extending 0.6 miles, offers an ideal spot for a refreshing swim and a dose of Andalusian sun. Afterward, you can enjoy lunch or drinks in one of the numerous excellent restaurants and bars along the nearby Paseo del Muelle Dos.

23. FERIA

Every August, typically around the middle of the month, Málaga's annual feria bursts into vibrant life. What sets Málaga's week-long celebration apart is that the festivities extend beyond the marquees, known as "casetas," situated on a sandy site the size of several football pitches, referred to as a "recinto." Unlike other major Andalusian cities, in Málaga, the daytime fiesta spills onto the streets. Spontaneous street parties erupt throughout the town, featuring women adorned in stunning flamenco dresses and groups of locals sharing bottles of cartojal, a sweet white wine that serves as the signature drink of the feria. Particularly lively areas include Calle Marques de Larios and Plaza de la Constitución in the old town, where locals gather for dancing, drinking, and socializing all day, every day, for a week. It's simply a wonderful experience.

24. BULLRING

To get the best views of Málaga's charming 19th-century bullring, head to the turrets of Gibralfaro castle. From there, you can observe the bullring nestled amidst high-rise apartment blocks just a short distance from the sea. Construction of this elegant plaza began in 1874, and it hosted its inaugural bullfight two years later. Today, it stands as one of the most significant bullrings in Andalusia, hosting prestigious bullfights during Easter and the lively August fiesta in Málaga. Visitors can take guided tours of the bullring, and it also features a museum that delves into the history of this controversial spectacle.

25. EL PERCHEL

El Perchel is a quaint and slightly worn neighborhood located between the Guadalmedina River to the east and the Maria Zambrano train station to the west, making it one of Málaga's oldest districts. It may be hard to believe that Perchel exists within the same city as the polished and sophisticated old town. However, this contrast offers a genuine glimpse into the city's past, portraying life before Málaga transformed into a major tourist destination. Historically a working-class neighborhood, El Perchel has maintained its authenticity, with many locals historically earning their livelihood from the nearby ocean. Today, it remains a go-to destination for those seeking the freshest fish in the city, available at stalls in the delightful Mercado del Carmen.

TOP 10 BEAUTIFUL BEACHES

Malaga's stunning beaches, cliffs, and bays are renowned for their beauty and draw visitors year-round with over 300 days of sunshine annually. Among the top attractions are the trendy beaches offering a plethora of activities. Many beachfront areas feature amenities such as restaurants, cafes, and bars, making them ideal spots for leisure and relaxation.

1. EL PALO BEACH

El Palo Beach, recognized as one of Malaga's finest, offers a family-friendly environment and boasts the Q Seal of Tourism Quality. Torremolinos' coastline, with its six main beaches connected by a lengthy promenade, is a favorite among both locals and tourists. La Caleta Beach stands out for its well-maintained dark sand and has been honored with the Blue Flag for Environmental Education.

2. TORREMOLINOS BEACHES

The beaches of Torremolinos are highly sought-after by both residents and visitors alike. Torremolinos boasts six primary beaches: Bajondillo, Los Alamos, Playamar, Montemar, La Carihuela, and El Saltillo. These beaches are linked by an extensive 8-kilometer (5-mile) promenade, providing easy access and scenic walks along the coastline. Among them, Playa de la Carihuela stands out as the largest beach in Torremolinos.

3. LA CALETA BEACH

La Caleta Beach, renowned for its impeccably maintained dark sand, is a standout coastal destination. Recognized for its environmental stewardship, the beach has been honored with the Blue Flag designation by the European Foundation for its commitment to environmental education. Stretching approximately 1 kilometer in length, the beach treats visitors to stunning vistas of the surrounding mountains. Amenities such as boat rentals, sunbeds, and umbrellas ensure a comfortable and enjoyable experience for beachgoers.

4. LA MISERICORDIA BEACH

La Misericordia Beach, characterized by its scenic dark sand, stretches approximately 2 kilometers in length and spans around 30 meters in width. Situated within the city limits of Malaga, this Blue Flag beach is known for its distinctive feature: an old industrial chimney situated adjacent to the shoreline. Additionally, it holds fame for being a prime location to witness the natural phenomenon known as the "Ola del Melillero."

5. GUADALMAR BEACH

Guadalmar Beach, also known as Playa de Guadalmar, is a stretch of dark sandy coastline measuring over 400 meters long, extending to the estuary of the Guadalhorce River. It is primarily frequented by naturists and holds the distinction of being Malaga's sole officially designated nudist beach. Notably, its proximity to Malaga airport means that low-flying aircraft are a frequent presence overhead.

6. EL DEDO BEACH (PLAYA EL DEDO)

El Dedo Beach, also known as Playa El Dedo or El Chanquete Beach, is a family-friendly coastline spanning approximately 550 meters in length and around 25 meters in width. It runs from El Palo beach to the Gálica Stream, reaching up to El Candado Marina. This beach, characterized by dark sand and featuring a promenade along its waterfront, has been honored with the Blue Flag distinction. One of its notable attractions is the unique dining experience offered by the El Tintero beach bar, renowned for its unconventional method of serving fish.

7. EL CANDADO BEACH

El Candado Beach, also known as Playa El Candado, is a compact private shoreline measuring just 200 meters in length. It is exclusively owned by the Club Náutico El Candado and is situated near the El Candado Marina. The beach boasts restaurants with terraces and tables, where patrons can indulge in a variety of traditional gourmet dishes.

8. LA MALAGUETA BEACH

La Malagueta Beach, positioned between the Port of Malaga and La Caleta Beach, stands as a favored destination for both locals and tourists alike. Stretching 1.2 kilometers in length and extending 45 meters wide, it offers moderate waves for beachgoers. This beach proudly bears the Blue Flag designation, signifying its cleanliness and safety standards. Easily reachable, La Malagueta Beach is adorned with a variety of dining options, including restaurants and bars, enhancing the visitor experience.

9. SAN JULIAN BEACH

San Julian Beach, also known as Playa de San Julián, is adjacent to a golf course, hence its name Campo de Golf San Julián Beach. As Malaga's largest beach, it spans approximately 2.5 kilometers in length, reaching from Los Alamos to the Guadalhorce River. Surrounded by greenery, this beach offers a tranquil atmosphere with relatively low crowds. It is particularly favored by kite surfers and provides ample space for activities such as football.

10. HUELIN BEACH

Huelin Beach, nestled between the San Andres and La Misericordia coastal areas, boasts a length of over 700 meters and a width of approximately 15 meters. With its dark sandy shores, this beach offers convenient access from the city center. Adjacent to the beach, visitors can explore attractions such as Huelin Park and the Antonio Machado Beachfront Promenade. Along the shoreline, numerous bars and restaurants cater to visitors, serving a variety of traditional dishes.

SIGHTSEEING & LANDMARKS

Malaga beckons you to explore its rich cultural and historical heritage through its array of sights and landmarks. From ancient marvels like the 13th-century Alcazaba to magnificent Baroque cathedrals and museums, the city offers a diverse tapestry of attractions. Beyond its historical treasures, Malaga boasts stunning vistas of the Costa de Sol and boasts beautiful beaches, parks, and gardens, providing ample opportunities for relaxation and enjoyment. Preserving its old-world charm while embracing modern values, Malaga's charming streets and splendid views captivate tourists and offer countless opportunities to capture memorable photographs.

MALAGA PARKS & GARDENS

The parks and gardens of Malaga are vibrant havens teeming with life! Scattered throughout the Costa del Sol, these green spaces invite exploration and relaxation. You can unwind beneath towering trees, serenaded by the melodies of chirping birds, or simply take leisurely strolls, inhaling the crisp, fresh air. Noteworthy parks like Malaga Park and La Batería Park showcase an array of exotic plant species sourced from diverse corners of the globe. Additionally, Malaga is home to several wildlife parks such as the Crocodile Park, which add an exciting dimension to holiday adventures. Lobo Park, offering guided tours, provides an immersive wildlife experience for visitors.

1. MALAGA PARK (PARQUE DE MALAGA)

Malaga Park, also known as Parque de Malaga, spans 3 hectares (30,000 sq.m.) of reclaimed land from the sea, dating back to the late 19th century. Stretching from Plaza del General Torrijos to Plaza de la Marina, this picturesque oasis boasts winding pathways, lush gardens adorned with roses, orange and palm trees, as well as exotic flora, fountains, and sculptures. It serves as an idyllic retreat from the city's hustle and bustle, inviting visitors to immerse themselves in the tranquility of nature. **Address:** Paseo del Parque, 29016 Malaga, Spain.

2. CROCODILE PARK (PARQUE DE COCODRILOS)

The Crocodile Park is situated in Torremolinos, nestled within the heart of the Costa del Sol. Here, visitors have the opportunity to encounter and marvel at prehistoric creatures that have thrived for over 200 million years of evolution. At the park, guests can stroll alongside these magnificent creatures, hold baby crocodiles in their hands, and capture unlimited photos to their heart's content—the adventure knows no bounds. **Address:** Calle Cuba, 14, 29620 Torremolinos, Malaga, Spain.

3. MONTES DE MALAGA NATURAL PARK (PARQUE NATURAL MONTES DE MÁLAGA)

The Montes de Malaga Natural Park, often referred to as the "green lung" of the city, encompasses a sprawling 4,996 hectares of verdant forest land. Situated on the northern outskirts of Malaga, within the heart of the Montes de Malaga coastal mountain range, this natural sanctuary boasts a rich tapestry of flora and fauna. The park is home to diverse tree species such as pines, cork oaks, scarlet oaks, and olive trees, among others. Its wildlife includes a variety of mammals like genets, badgers, and foxes, as well as reptiles such as the ocellated lizard and the Mediterranean chameleon. Birds of prey such as eagles and Eurasian sparrowhawks also inhabit the area. | **Address:** Casabermeja-Colmenar, Malaga, Spain.

4. LOBO PARK

Lobo Park offers visitors a unique opportunity to observe wolves in their semi-natural environment. Nestled in the heart of Andalusia, in Antequera, this park is home to four species of wolves, including the indigenous Iberian wolves. Lobo Park conducts guided tours where knowledgeable guides provide insights into these magnificent creatures and their natural behaviors. | **Address:** Carr. de Antequera, km 16, 29200 Antequera, Malaga, Spain.

5. BATERÍA PARK (PARQUE LA BATERÍA)

The urban park, commonly referred to as Battery Park, acts as a vital green space within the city of Torremolinos. It encompasses a variety of features including a lookout tower, gardens, numerous pathways, a man-made lake, a children's playground, a dedicated bike path, and decorative fountains. With its diverse flora and fauna, Batería Park is a beloved destination for both tourists and locals alike. **Address:** Avenida del Carmelo, s/n, 29620 Torremolinos, Málaga, Spain.

7. JARDÍN BOTÁNICO-HISTÓRICO LA CONCEPCIÓN

Dating back to the mid-19th century, the gardens showcase an impressive array of fauna and flora, featuring trees from five continents, over 49 hectares of tropical forest, and 23 hectares of botanical gardens. Spring, considered the optimal time to visit, transforms the gardens with vibrant colors and captivating scents from the blooming exotic specimens, creating an illusion of being in a distant tropical land rather than on the outskirts of one of Europe's most popular cities. The garden is particularly renowned for its collection of palm trees, some of which are over a century old, along with a 400-year-old olive tree. | To reach the Botanical Garden, catch either bus number 2 or 91, then enjoy a brief stroll to your destination. Visit their website at *laconcepcion.malaga.eu* | **Free Admission:** all day on Sundays from Oct. 1st to March 31st, Sundays from 15:00 to 16:30 throughout the rest of the year | **Address:** Camino del Jardín Botánico, 3. | *Opening Hours:* Mon:

NICHOLASINGRAM

Closed, Tue – Sun: 9:30 – 16:30.

CRUISING MALAGA

If you're dreaming of sailing in the bay of Malaga, your voyage begins at Malaga port, a bustling hub that welcomes a significant number of cruise ships annually. Ranked as the second largest cruise port in the Peninsula after Barcelona, Malaga port has recently undergone a major refurbishment, transforming it into a beautiful Mediterranean Marina. Conveniently located just 1.5 kilometers from the historic center of Malaga, the port is easily accessible from the railway station, bus station, and airport, all within a short distance. Moreover, it serves as a gateway to the Balearic Islands, French coast, and African coasts.

Planning and booking your cruise can be daunting with numerous options available online. Below are tips to help you plan and book your dream cruise:

1. Decide on your desired destination area from the wide range of choices available. | 2. Book your cruise through a specialist to ensure you select the right one for you. | 3. Book in advance to secure the best deals and discounts. | 4. Choose a package that fits your budget and carefully review what is included. | 5. Prepare for inclement weather by packing essential items.

With these tips in mind, you can embark on an unforgettable cruise adventure and make your dream vacation a reality.

TOP 10 MUST-VISIT MUSEUMS

Over time, Malaga has emerged as a significant hub for cultural and artistic heritage. In addition to its wealth of historical buildings and monuments, the city boasts an array of museums and art galleries showcasing incredible artworks. In the past 15 years, the museum scene has flourished, solidifying Malaga's reputation as a city of museums. To assist you in navigating this rich cultural landscape, we've curated a list of the top 10 museums in Malaga that are essential stops during your visit. Furthermore, we'll provide some helpful insights to enhance your museum-going experience. Malaga boasts a total of 37 museums, spanning a diverse range from archaeology to modern art. With such a variety, there's something to captivate every visitor's interest. **TIPS:** If you're an art enthusiast eager to explore multiple museums without breaking the bank, consider planning your visits for Sunday. Many of Malaga's museums offer free admission on Sundays. For specific details on free entry hours, refer to our blog post for comprehensive information.

1. PICASSO MUSEUM

The Pablo Ruiz Picasso Museum in Malaga celebrates the life and work of the renowned artist, offering a rich collection of over 200 artworks that trace his evolution as an artist from his early pieces to his masterpieces. The museum also hosts temporary exhibitions to provide fresh perspectives on Picasso's legacy. Located near his birthplace at Plaza de la Merced, visiting the museum offers insight into the artist's upbringing, with nearby streets offering a glimpse into the neighborhood that influenced him. Visitors can enjoy a coffee at the museum's cafeteria, surrounded by pigeons—a motif significant in Picasso's and his father's artwork. Exploring the vicinity further, tourists can find charming streets, traditional eateries, shops, and wine bars, with recommendations for iconic spots like Cortijo de Pepe, known for its authentic Andalusian cuisine. | **OPENING HOURS:** *September-October, March-June:* Daily from 10:00 to 19:00 | **November-February:** Daily from 10:00 to 18:00 | **July-August:** Daily from 10:00 to 20:00 | **Ticket Prices**: Collection: €9 (Reduced*: €7) | **Temporary Exhibition:** €8 (Reduced*: €6) | **Combined:** €12 (Reduced*: €9) | (*Reduced fees apply to European Youth Card holders, students under 26 with valid ID, and visitors over 65.) | **Website:** museopicassomalaga.org | **Address:** Palacio de Buenavista, Calle San Agustín, 8.

2. CARMEN THYSSEN MUSEUM

The Carmen Thyssen Museum showcases a remarkable selection from the private collection of Carmen Thyssen-Bornemisza, primarily focusing on Spanish and Andalusian paintings from the 19th century. This gallery offers a captivating journey through various styles of Spanish painting, with a particular emphasis on Andalusian artists such as Julio Romero de Torres, Joaquín Sorolla, and Aureliano de Beruete. With over 2,600 works, the extensive collection provides a comprehensive overview of 19th-century Spanish art. *Exploring the museum*, you'll encounter artworks depicting Easter week, the Feria, and the vibrant essence of Andalusian cities—a testament to the region's rich cultural heritage. The Thyssen Museum also hosts temporary exhibitions, enriching the visitor's experience with diverse artistic perspectives. | **OPENING HOURS:** Tuesday to Sunday, from 10:00 to 20:00

Ticket Prices: *Normal Ticket:* €10 | *Reduced Ticket:* €6 | **Website:** *carmenthyssenmalaga.org* | **Address:** Calle Compañía, 10.

3. CENTRE POMPIDOU

Another unmissable museum on our list is the Centre Pompidou Malaga, marking the first expansion of the renowned modern art institution outside of France. Situated near the port in a distinctive building known as El Cubo (the cube), the gallery stands out with its vibrant and colorful rooftop structure—a notable landmark in Malaga. Inside, visitors can explore the semi-permanent exhibition "Modern Utopias" (available until the end of 2020) and a rotating program of temporary exhibitions. | **OPENING HOURS:** 9:30 to 20:00, closed on Tuesdays | **TICKET PRICES:** Permanent Exhibition: €7 (Reduced: €4)* | Temporary Exhibition: €4 (Reduced: €2.50)* | Combined: €9 (Reduced: €2.50)* | (*Reduced rates available for students under 26, seniors over 65, and large families) | **WEBSITE:** *https://centrepompidou-malaga.eu* | **Address:** Pasaje Doctor Carrillo Casaux, s/n, 29016 Muelle Uno, Puerto de Málaga

4. MUSEUM OF MALAGA

Housed within the splendid Palacio de Aduana, the Museum of Malaga is a treasure trove of archaeological and historical artifacts, boasting a collection of over 17,000 exhibits. Through its permanent exhibition, the museum offers a captivating journey through the history of Malaga, showcasing artifacts from various civilizations that have shaped the region, including the Phoenicians, Romans, Visigoths, and Muslims. Additionally, the museum's upper floor features a remarkable collection of 19th and 20th-century paintings. As the largest museum in Andalusia and the fifth largest in Spain, the Museum of Malaga offers an immersive exploration of the region's rich cultural heritage. | **OPENING HOURS** (*Winter, 16 September to 15 June*): Tuesday to Saturday: 9:00 to 20:00 | Sundays and Holidays: 9:00 to 15:00 | *Opening Hours (Summer, 16 June to 15 September):* Tuesday to Saturday: 9:00 to 21:00 | Sunday: 9:00 to 15:00 | **Tickets:** €1.50 / Free for EU citizens | **Website:** museosdeandalucia.es | **Address:** Plaza de la Aduana, S/N.

5. REVELLO DE TORO MUSEUM

Dedicated to the lives and artistic legacies of Revello de Toro, a renowned portrait painter from Malaga, and Pedro de Mena, a skilled creator of religious sculptures, this museum is housed within a 17th-century residence formerly owned by de Toro himself. The exhibition boasts over 100 paintings, sketches, and drawings by Revello de Toro, celebrated primarily for his evocative portraits, particularly those portraying sensuous female subjects. A highlight of the museum is the Memorial Room, where visitors can view a captivating 10-minute video showcasing the life and accomplishments of the former homeowner. Be sure to stay until the end for a surprising conclusion! | **OPENING HOURS:** *Tuesday to Saturday*: 10:00 to 20:00, *Sunday:* 10:00 to 14:00 | *Ticket Prices*: Normal: €2.50 | *Groups (5 or more people):* €2 | *Minors under 18 and seniors over 65:* Free | **Website:** museorevellodetoro.net | *Address*: Calle Afligidos, 5.

6. RUSSIAN MUSEUM

As the inaugural European outpost of the State Russian Museum, this museum in Malaga showcases a curated selection of 100 artworks spanning the 15th to 20th centuries, offering a comprehensive survey of Russian artistic movements. The museum features a rotating annual exhibition, providing visitors with insight into various periods of Russian and Soviet art. Housed within a historic 1920s tobacco factory, the museum's architecture and decor add to the immersive experience. | **OPENING HOURS:** *Tuesday to Sunday:* 9:30 to 20:00 | **Ticket Prices:** *Annual Exhibition*: €6 (Reduced:

€3.50)* | *Temporary Exhibition:* €4 (Reduced: €2.50)* | *Combined Ticket:* €8 (Reduced: €4)* | (*Reduced rates apply to seniors over 65 and students under 26. For free admission, please refer to the website.) | **Website:** www.coleccionmuseoruso.es | **Address:** Edificio de Tabacalera, Av de Sor Teresa Prat, 15.

7. WINE MUSEUM

Acknowledging the integral role of red wine in Spanish culture and cuisine, the Malaga Wine Museum celebrates the region's rich viticultural heritage. Benefiting from Andalusia's geology, warm climate, and centuries-old winemaking traditions, the museum showcases wines of exceptional quality, offering visitors insights into various grape varieties, winemaking techniques, and production processes. A highlight of the visit is the complimentary wine tasting experience, allowing guests to savor the flavors of local vintages. | **Opening Hours:** Monday to Friday: 10:00-17:00, Saturday: 10:00-14:00 | **Tickets:** €5, with discounts available for students, children, seniors, and groups. | **Website:** *http://www.museovinomalaga.com* | **Address:** Plaza de la Aduana, S/N.

8. AUTOMOBILE AND FASHION MUSEUM

A captivating fusion of automotive history and high fashion, the Malaga Automobile and Fashion Museum presents an impressive collection of over 90 exclusive automobiles, showcasing the aesthetic evolution of cars throughout the 20th century. From iconic brands like Jaguar, Porsche, Rolls Royce, to Aston Martin, visitors can admire some of the world's most renowned vehicles. Complementing the automotive display is a stunning array of luxury fashion, featuring exquisite garments from esteemed designers such as Chanel, Dior, Prada, and Balmain. Housed within the historic confines of an old tobacco factory in Huelin, the museum offers a captivating experience for enthusiasts of both automobiles and fashion. | **Opening Hours:** Monday to Sunday: 10:00-19:00 | **Tickets:** Normal: €9.50, Seniors: €7, Reduced: €5 | **Website:** *https://www.museoautomovilmalaga.com* | **Address:** Edificio de La Tabacalera, en Avenida Sor Teresa Prat 15.

9. CENTER OF CONTEMPORARY ART MALAGA (CAC)

Dedicated to showcasing 20th and 21st-century visual art encompassing paintings, sculptures, photography, and videography, the Center of Contemporary Art Malaga (CAC) offers a dynamic space for exploring both

permanent and temporary exhibitions featuring works by national and local artists. Situated in the vibrant Soho neighborhood, the CAC invites visitors to immerse themselves in a diverse array of contemporary artistic expressions. | **Opening Hours:**
Winter (Tuesday to Sunday): 10:00 – 20:00 | **Summer (Tuesday to Sunday):** 10:00 – 14:00 and 17:00 – 21:00 | **Tickets:** Free Entry | **Address:** Calle Alemanía, s/n | **Website:** *http://cacmalaga.eu*

10. MUSEUM OF MUNICIPAL HERITAGE

Rounding out our list of top museums in Malaga is the Museum of Municipal Heritage, offering a comprehensive collection focused on local painting, sculpture, culture, and history. With a compilation of 400 pieces spanning from the 15th to the 20th century, the museum provides a fascinating journey through the evolution of the city and its artistic heritage. Additionally, the museum regularly hosts temporary exhibitions, ensuring there's always something new to discover. | **Opening Hours:** Tuesday to Sunday: 10:00 – 20:00 | **Tickets:** Free Entry | **Website:** *http://museodelpatrimoniomunicipal.malaga.eu* | **Address:** Paseo Reding, 1

15 MALAGA CITY HIDDEN GEMS

This section explore some hidden gems and secret spots in Malaga city. However, the entire Malaga region is also filled with incredible and lesser-known landmarks and marvels.

1. CAMINITO DEL REY

If you're up for a hike, we highly recommend exploring the Caminito del Rey. This 8-kilometer trail offers breathtaking views, elevated almost 100 meters above the bottom of the gorge through which the river runs. The trail is situated between the towns of Álora, Antequera, and Ardales in the Desfiladero de los Gaitanes gorge. Constructed over 100 years ago as a passage for workers of two hydroelectric plants, this trail promises an unforgettable experience. Due to safety reasons, it's essential to book entrance tickets in advance, as the number of hikers per day is limited. Wearing a helmet is also mandatory. The Caminito del Rey is located 30 kilometers north of Málaga, making it perfect for a day trip.

2. MONTE SAN ANTÓN

Monte San Antón is the ideal spot in town to witness a breathtaking sunset. Situated in the eastern part of the city of Málaga, it stands out as one of the impressive viewpoints along the Costa del Sol. At the mountain's summit, you'll find the San Antón Cross, offering a magnificent panoramic view of the city with the Mediterranean Sea as a stunning backdrop. To enhance your experience, consider purchasing some goodies from the local markets to create a delicious picnic and bring along a good bottle of wine. This way, you can fully savor the sunset in this picturesque setting.

3. LA CASA INVISIBLE

La Casa Invisible, nestled in Malaga's historical center, is a unique cultural and community hub founded in 2007. Housed in a renovated 19th-century palace, it offers a charming courtyard for affordable drinks and snacks. Beyond that, it serves as a self-managed space for cultural expression, social activism, and community involvement. With a diverse range of events, workshops, and projects, it provides a platform for local and international talent while fostering dialogue on social and environmental issues. The venue's relaxed atmosphere, adorned with colorful murals, offers a tranquil escape. Despite facing challenges and protests in February 2024, La Casa Invisible remains a must-visit for those seeking an authentic cultural experience in Malaga. Visitors are advised to check the website or social media for updates on events and opening hours. | **Website:** *https://www-lainvisible.net* | **IG:** *https://www.instagram.com/lacasainvisible*

4. LA CONCEPCION - OFF THE TOURIST PATH BOTANICAL GARDEN

La Concepcion Botanical Garden in the northern part of the city is a place that not many tourists visit, even though it is featured in many guidebooks. The reason might be that few people appreciate the value of botanical gardens. Nevertheless, I believe you'll love this place as its expansive area features not only a diverse array of plants but also numerous sculptures, fountains, and other decorative elements. Visiting feels like entering an oasis with collections of palms, bamboo, cacti, and water lilies. Parts of the garden even evoke a sense of Bali or another jungle-like setting. The plants come from around the world, including tropical and subtropical species.

The Marquis and Marchioness of Loring, passionate about plants and gardening in the mid-19th century, created La Concepcion on the same territory where they had a house. Besides its extensive plant collections, the garden offers amenities such as guided tours, long walking paths, educational programs, and a cafe. It's easy to spend half a day here without noticing how quickly time passes. You don't need to be a fan of plants or gardening to appreciate this gem. If you enjoy spending time in beautiful outdoor spaces, a visit to La Concepcion Botanical Garden is special. It stands as one of the most important and impressive botanical gardens in Spain, a must-see attraction for visitors to Malaga. It also offers some pretty views of Malaga city! Check prices and schedules on the La Concepcion website - Website: . If your trip falls on a Sunday, expect free entrance to the garden.

5. PEÑA JUAN BREVA FLAMENCO MUSEUM & BAR

The next Malaga hidden gem is a place that will be of particular interest to those who love flamenco. Peña Juan Breva Flamenco Museum & Bar is a cultural center, museum, and bar all in one. Dedicated to the art of flamenco, a traditional style of music and dance popular in Andalusia, this museum is a cool spot to learn about flamenco shows and watch some of the best flamenco performances in Malaga. The museum is named after Juan Breva, a famous flamenco singer from Malaga who lived in the 19th and early 20th centuries. It features a collection of artifacts related to flamenco, including costumes, instruments, and photographs. Interactive exhibits allow visitors to learn about the history and culture of this art form. While the museum itself is small and takes a maximum of one hour to explore, it is interesting and informative, especially for those new to flamenco. The highlight of this gem is the bar and underground performance room where visitors can enjoy live flamenco shows accompanied by tapas and traditional drinks. The decorations, done in a traditional style with colorful tiles and artwork, create a festive atmosphere. To watch a show, make a reservation at least a few days in advance as the place is popular among locals. I recommend going there directly to make a reservation on the spot if you don't speak Spanish. If you do, it's better to call them, as Señor Paco usually responds to calls and is very helpful.

6. LAGUNILLAS NEIGHBORHOOD - CENTER OF STREET ART IN MALAGA

The Lagunillas neighborhood in Málaga, located just a short walk from the city's historic part and main tourist attractions, is not home to major museums or cultural institutions. However, its vibrant street art, quirky shops, and alternative culture make it a cool destination for those seeking something off the beaten path. The street art scene in Lagunillas began in the early 2000s when local artists started using the neighborhood's walls as their canvas. This turned it into a hub for street art in Malaga, drawing artists from around the world to leave their mark on its walls. In addition to its street art, Lagunillas is known for its alternative vibe. The neighborhood features independent shops, bars, and cafes and is home to a diverse community of artists, musicians, and other creatives. While exploring Lagunillas, consider buying traditional homemade Spanish food, mainly takeout, from a local shop like _La Oliva Negra_. Alternatively, venture a bit farther to _El Ombu Empanadas_ to try amazing Argentinian empanadas. For those craving southern Italy cuisine, _SAN Sabor restaurant_ is a favorite spot. If you haven't chosen accommodation yet, consider staying in the Lagunillas neighborhood for an alternative experience, like at _Hotel Bro_, which offers some rooms with pools.

7. MERCADO DE SALAMANCA

Mercado de Salamanca is a fresh produce market not widely known among tourists but popular among locals. Here, you can experience local culture and cuisine while witnessing the lively and bustling market life reminiscent of the past. The market offers a wide variety of fruits, vegetables, meats, seafood, and cheeses. Though relatively small, it has a vibrant atmosphere where visitors can sample fresh seafood and traditional dishes like paella, tapas, and fried fish. If you're not planning to shop for fresh produce, you can still enjoy fried fish and tapas at the market's cafes. Prices here are often lower than at Mercado Central, and the vendors are friendly and ready to help you choose the right products. The butchers' section includes intriguing products made on-site, such as salchichas and fresh chorizos. Even if you don't intend to do fresh produce shopping, a visit to Mercado de Salamanca is worthwhile for its Moorish-influenced exterior and interior, adding another layer of cultural richness to the experience.

8. ROOFTOP OF THE CATEDRAL DE LA ENCARNACIÓN

While the Catedral de la Encarnación itself is not a hidden gem, its rooftop is often discovered only after visiting the cathedral, making it a must-visit in Malaga. The cathedral, one of the most impressive Gothic cathedrals in Spain, offers a unique perspective of the city from its rooftop. From the top, visitors can enjoy panoramic views of the Old City, the sea, and the surrounding mountains, providing an excellent opportunity for photography. If you're comfortable with heights and stairs, the guided rooftop tours, starting at 11:00 and continuing every hour until 18:00, offer a memorable experience. Find information about entrance fees and guidelines on the cathedral's official website here -

9. HOTEL CASTILLO DE SANTA CATALINA
FOR DRINKS, SUNSET & VIEWS

Hotel Castillo De Santa Catalina is a hidden gem boutique hotel in Malaga that goes beyond being a place to stay; it's a unique destination worth a visit. Housed in a 1932 castle built in the neo-Mudéjar style, combining Islamic and Spanish Renaissance elements, the hotel sits atop a hill, providing stunning views of Malaga's port, the Mediterranean Sea, and prestigious neighborhoods. Originally a private residence, the castle was opened as a hotel in 1971 after extensive renovations. Even if you're not staying overnight, you can visit as an outside guest to enjoy a meal or a drink in the cozy restaurant, gaining access to the beautiful grounds. The hotel's restaurant, situated in a lush garden with a terrace, offers gorgeous sunset views and is considered one of the best places to watch sunsets in Malaga. Whether for a romantic dinner or drinks, Hotel Castillo De Santa Catalina provides a unique and memorable experience.

Note: It's advisable to check the hotel's website or contact them directly for the most up-to-date information on dining options, reservations, and access for non-staying guests.

10. EL MAYORAZGO NEIGHBORHOOD & LA CHEESEQUERIA WITH BEST CHEESECAKES IN MALAGA

La Cheesequeria is a hidden gem in Malaga, located in the El Mayorazgo neighborhood, and is a must-visit destination, especially if you have a sweet tooth. The El Mayorazgo neighborhood itself is known for its tranquil atmosphere, hilly streets with traditional Spanish architecture, whitewashed walls, red-tiled roofs, and several parks and gardens, making it a unique area to explore if you are staying longer in Malaga. La Cheesequeria specializes in cheesecakes that stand out with their unique, liquidish, pudding-like filling that melts in your mouth. The cafe offers a delightful and different cheesecake experience compared to the traditional ones. If you're in the neighborhood, a stop at La Cheesequeria is highly recommended for a sweet treat.

11. LESSER-KNOWN MUSEUM OF WINE

While Malaga is renowned for its art museums, the Lesser-known Museum of Wine offers a distinct and fascinating perspective, dedicated to the history and culture of wine in the Malaga region. Situated in the historic city center, the museum occupies a beautifully restored 18th-century palace, adding to its charm. Although the museum is small, it provides a comprehensive look at the wine-making process, covering everything from grape cultivation to bottling and aging. Exhibits showcase different grape varieties in the region, the history of wine-making in Malaga, and various wine types, including sweet wines like Pedro Ximenez and Moscatel. You can engage in guided tours, tastings, and workshops (it's advisable to inquire in advance as they are not daily) to delve deeper into the techniques and traditions of wine-making passed down through generations. Additionally, there's a wine shop where guests can purchase a bottle of wine or wine-related souvenirs. Tucked away on a quieter street, this museum offers a unique and enriching experience for wine enthusiasts.

12. MALAGA HIDDEN BEACH EL PEÑÓN DEL CUERVO

If you're in Malaga and looking to escape the crowded city beach, El Peñón del Cuervo offers a beautiful and secluded alternative. Situated on the eastern outskirts of Malaga, near the hidden gem neighborhood of El Palo, this relatively small beach spans approximately 100 meters and boasts a unique landscape and serene atmosphere. El Peñón del Cuervo is surrounded by rocky cliffs and lush vegetation, providing a picturesque backdrop for photos and offering stunning views. The late afternoon or sunset is considered the best time to visit, with the beach offering a tranquil and peaceful experience compared to the more crowded city beaches. | *To reach El Peñón del Cuervo*, you can use public transport, hire a car, or even rent a bike for a more adventurous journey. Before heading to the beach, consider making a stop in one of the ***chirinquitos*** in El Palo for seafood with mesmerizing sea views. Notable options include **New Varadero** and **Restaurante Narval**. The beach area also provides amenities such as a small supermarket, public restrooms, and the option to rent sun loungers and umbrellas.

13. PEDREGALEJO & EL PALO – MORE MALAGA HIDDEN NEIGHBORHOODS

Continuing from El Peñón del Cuervo beach, the neighborhoods of Pedregalejo and El Palo are hidden gems in southern Spain, known for their traditional fishing village feel, fish restaurants, and quieter beaches. These neighborhoods have preserved their history as fishing communities, evident in the authentic seafood cafes, fishermen's houses, and fish markets. In summer, Pedregalejo and El Palo attract visitors with their beaches featuring black sand, ideal for swimming, sunbathing, and water sports. The evenings in these neighborhoods come alive with vibrant nightlife, offering numerous bars with affordable prices, popular among young people and students. If you seek the best seafood experience in Malaga, Pedregalejo and El Palo, located in the eastern part of the city, are excellent choices. Besides savoring delicious seafood at more reasonable prices than in Malaga city center, you can immerse yourself in traditional Andalusian life and enjoy access to lovely beaches.

14. SANTUARIO DE LA VICTORIA

Santuario de la Victoria is a beautiful Catholic church located in the historic

Conde de Urena neighborhood. You can visit it right after exploring the street-art neighborhood of Lagunillas. Built in the 17th century in the Baroque style, this church holds historical significance and stands out as one of the most important churches in Malaga city, showcasing stunning Baroque architecture. The exterior of the church is ornate, featuring intricate stonework and a large central dome. However, the real beauty lies in its interior, where impressive works of art, curved lines, and the use of light and shadow create a dramatic and awe-inspiring atmosphere. If you have the opportunity to visit Santuario de la Victoria during *Semana Santa (Holy Week)*, it offers a memorable experience. The church serves as the starting point for several important processions during this time, attracting people from all over Europe. | ***Opening Hours:*** The usual opening hours for the church are from 9:00 to 13:00 and between 17:00 and 19:00. It is recommended to explore the interior, especially the chapel leading to the second floor and altar, accessed through a spiral staircase. The chapel and altar boast ornate decorations, including gold leaf, intricate carvings, and colorful frescoes. At the center, you'll find a statue of the Virgen de la Victoria, the patron saint of Malaga, holding significant religious importance in the city.

15. HIDDEN AUTOMOBILE & FASHION MUSEUM

The Hidden Automobile & Fashion Museum is another unique and off-the-beaten-path destination in Malaga. Located away from the tourist paths, this museum showcases a remarkable collection of 90 special automotive displays, providing insights into the tasteful development of automobiles throughout the twentieth century. Beyond the cars, the museum features an impressive collection of designer clothes from renowned brands such as Chanel, Prada, Dior, and Balmain, spanning different eras in fashion history. You can explore vintage clothing and accessories, including dresses, hats, and jewelry, offering a captivating glimpse into the evolving fashion trends in Spain and beyond. Situated in the Old Tobacco Factory in the Huelin neighborhood, the Malaga Automobile and Fashion Museum is a hidden gem often overlooked by many tourists. Despite being on many lists of the world's best museums, it maintains a quiet and peaceful atmosphere, making it a unique and rewarding visit for enthusiasts of cars and fashion. It's a great place for couples or families with kids, and you can book your ticket in advance to secure a spot.

NICHOLAS INGRAM

SECRET COURTYARDS AND CHARMING PLAZAS

Indulging in a beach day is delightful, but venturing beyond the shore unveils a side of Spain filled with rich history and beauty. Below, we present five of the most captivating plazas in Málaga.

1. PLAZA OCHAVADA, ARCHIDONA

Located in the northern part of Málaga province, Archidona is a picturesque rural town known for its unique square, Plaza Ochavada. With an octagonal shape, each side boasts distinct architectural influences, inspired by the Renaissance in Italy's Siena. The plaza incorporates caves into its hillside, and notable among them is the renowned restaurant Arxiduna. Archidona, along with nearby Antequera, is a worthwhile day trip destination.

2. PLAZA DE LOS NARANJOS, MARBELLA

Dating back to 1485, Plaza de los Naranjos is nestled in Marbella's old town. Surrounded by historic buildings and typical white Andalucian structures, the plaza features a Renaissance fountain and orange trees, evoking the essence of the old town. While it offers a charming atmosphere with bars and restaurants, caution is advised regarding tourist trap prices.

3. PLAZA DE LA MERCED, MÁLAGA

Formerly Plaza del Mercado and later Plaza de Riego, Plaza de la Merced derives its current name from a church and convent. The central neo-classical obelisk commemorates the sacrifices made for patriotic liberty in 1831. Adorned with jacaranda trees, the square also hosts a statue of Picasso near the house of his birth. Bars and restaurants lining the square provide a perfect vantage point to savor the surroundings.

4. PLAZA DEL SOCORRO, RONDA

Renovated in 2019, Plaza del Socorro in Ronda holds political significance in Andalucía. The square features a statue of Hercules, moved from the fountain, and the church of Socorro of Ronda on one side. It witnessed a historic event in 1918 when Blas Infante unveiled the flag and emblem of Andalucía. The plaza resonates with the history of Ronda and Andalucía.

5. PLAZA ALMIJARA, CÓMPETA

Known as 'the pearl of the Axarquia,' Cómpeta is situated in the eastern mountains of Málaga. At its center lies Plaza Almijara, adorned with the

Church of Nuestra Senora de la Asuncion. The church's Neo-Mudejar tower, adorned with gold decoration, is a symbolic monument. The plaza, buzzing with bars and restaurants, showcases the town's history and traditions through the Paseo de las Tradiciones tiles.

Step away from the beaches and immerse yourself in the charm and history these plazas offer across Málaga.

CHAPTER 4: SAVORING THE LOCAL FLAVORS

FOOD IN MALAGA

Social gatherings, family occasions, cultural celebrations – in the stunning region of Andalusia, food is intertwined with every aspect of life! Visiting Malaga is an opportunity to embark on a culinary journey through the city's finest bars, restaurants, cafes, and chiringuitos (beach bars) in the city center and the casco antiguo, Málaga's old town. Below are some must-try food and drink options in Malaga:

Fresh Seafood: With its coastal location, Malaga offers a plethora of seafood delights. From espetos (grilled sardine skewers cooked over open fires on the beach) to boquerones (fried anchovies) and a variety of shellfish, there's something for every seafood enthusiast.

Tapas: As is customary in much of Spain, tapas reign supreme in Malaga. From classic offerings like olives & almonds to more elaborate local specialties such as flamenquín (breaded and fried meat, typically ham & pork) and salmorejo (a chilled tomato & bread soup akin to gazpacho), the diversity of Malaga's tapas scene is a true delight.

Churros with Chocolate: Malaga's claim to fame in the realm of sweets is undoubtedly churros with chocolate. These fried dough pastries, served with a thick, velvety hot chocolate for dipping, are a beloved breakfast or snack option.

Malaga Wine: Renowned for its sweet wine varieties, particularly Moscatel, Malaga offers a delightful array of wine options to complement your culinary journey.

Albóndigas en Salsa de Almendras: Reflecting the Moorish influence on Andalusian cuisine, albóndigas (meatballs) in almond sauce are a delectable specialty not to be missed.

Whether you're savoring fresh catches from the sea, delighting in the art of tapas, indulging in sweet treats, or raising a glass of local wine, Malaga promises a culinary adventure like no other.

25 MUST-TRY LOCAL DISHES

Malaga boasts a distinctive culinary scene, showcasing a variety of indigenous delicacies like olives, almonds, grapes, raisins, sweet wine, olive oil, seafood, fresh produce, and delectable pastries, you'll never struggle to decide what to eat as the local culinary scene caters to a wide range of preferences, including meat lovers, vegans, fish aficionados, and vegetarians. Embracing local cuisine enhances the dining pleasures, and with an array of flavorful offerings, it's hard to resist. To guarantee you savor equally delightful culinary adventures during your visit, below are 25 quintessential Malaguenan dishes you simply shouldn't miss when you are in Malaga:

1. ESPETOS – SARDINE SKEWERS

Espetos, a beloved delicacy in Malaga, are sardine skewers typically grilled on the beach or on specialized boats for outdoor barbecues. These skewers, usually made of bamboo, can hold up to six sardines at a time. Best savored between May and August, numerous beachfront chiringuitos (beach bars) in Malaga and surrounding areas serve this quintessential Andalusian dish. Legend has it that chef Miguel Martinez Soler, also known as Miguel, el de las Sardinas (Miguel the Sardine Man), introduced the modern preparation of espetos to King Alfonso XII in 1884. | **_Best Place to Sample Espetos:_** El Tintero in El Palo, Malaga

2. FRITURA MALAGUEÑA – FRIED FISH

Fritura Malagueña is a beloved traditional dish hailing from Malaga, featuring an assortment of small fried fish, shellfish, and crustaceans. Common varieties include sardines, anchovies, squid, shrimp, and sometimes even small crabs or octopus. The dish is usually accompanied by lemon wedges for a citrusy kick and aioli, a creamy mayonnaise infused with garlic, adding richness and flavor. This culinary delight captures the essence of Malaga's coastal cuisine, offering a delightful combination of flavors and textures. | **_Best Place to Sample_** Los Mellizos

3. GAZPACHUELO MALAGUEÑO

Gazpachuelo Malagueño is a staple dish found in all reputable restaurants in Malaga. Distinct from the typical cold gazpacho tomato soup – a misconception I've learned from firsthand experience. Although it's a soup, Gazpachuelo Malagueño contains none of the ingredients found in gazpacho.

Made with mayonnaise, egg yolk, hake, and prawns, this dish is a traditional favorite among fishermen, falling into the "love it or hate it" category of Malagueñan cuisine – certainly not everyone's preference. | **_Best Place to Sample_**: Restaurante Alexso

4. PORRA ANTEQUERANA

While Porra Antequerana belongs to the gazpacho family, it differs from the refreshing cold tomato soup typically enjoyed during scorching summers. Named after the nearby city of Antequera, Porra Antequerana is notably thicker and mainly comprised of tomatoes and dried bread crumbs. Unlike gazpacho, Porra Antequerana is commonly served as a tapa rather than an appetizer. | **_Best Place to Sample_**: La Mejillonería

5. ENSALADA MALAGUEÑA

Ensalada malagueña is a refreshing potato salad featuring bacalao (cod) and oranges as its main components. The people of Malaga, known as boquerones, certainly know how to make the most of their favorite fish variety, and this summer salad is undoubtedly a highlight. | **_Best Place to Sample_**: El Pimpi

6. MALAGA WINE

The premier bars in Malaga's historic district also boast the finest selections of the city's renowned wines. Whether you crave a Tinto Verano or seek a house wine offering a symphony of aromas and flavors, the casco antiguo is the go-to destination for wine aficionados seeking the finest picks. | **_Best Place to Sample_**: Antigua Casa de Guardia

7. TARTA MALAGUEÑA

Crafted exclusively from local ingredients, Tarta Malagueña is an almond-based confection soaked in moscatel wine, infused with cinnamon, studded with raisins, and often adorned with homemade apricot jam. This dessert represents one of the most exquisite Andalusian treats to savor in Malaga. | **_Best Place to Sample_**: Dulces Dreams Boutique Hostel & Cafe Gallery

8. COFFEE MALAGA STYLE

A visit to Malaga offers an education in coffee, introducing an array of unique styles you may not have encountered before. To aid in your selection, most cafes and bars display the Café Central poster, a visual guide showcasing options like café solo, largo, semi largo, solo corto, mitad, entre corto, corto, and sombra, ensuring your coffee experience aligns precisely with your preferences. For the ultimate coffee experience, visit Café con Libros for a cuppa and a perusal. | ***Best Place to Sample***: Café con Libros Café Central

9. ALMENDRAS FRITAS

Few aromas rival the enticing scent of almendras fritas – almonds fried to perfection in sunflower oil. Whether enjoyed as a bar snack or savored at the annual feria, they offer an authentic taste of Andalusia. For the most delectable almendras fritas, venture to one of Malaga city's finest dining establishments, notably the aptly named Restaurante Bienmesabe, which translates to "it tastes good," also alluding to a special fish dish. | ***Best Place to Sample***: Restaurante Bienmesabe

10. BOQUERONES AL LIMÓN

Boquerones al Limón is a classic Andalusian dish featuring fresh anchovies marinated in lemon juice, olive oil, garlic, and parsley. The acidity of the lemon juice helps "cook" the fish, giving it a tender texture and imparting a bright, citrusy flavor. It's typically served as a tapa or appetizer, accompanied by crusty bread to soak up the flavorful marinade. This dish showcases the simple yet delicious flavors of the Mediterranean. Embark on your Malaga adventure by indulging in boquerones al limón – whether on the beach, in the city, or within the casco antiguo. Regardless of the setting, Malaga offers the freshest and most expertly prepared boquerones al limón, showcasing the city's unparalleled love for anchovies. Malagueñan chefs excel in perfecting this dish, making it a must-try. | ***Best Place to Sample***: La Peregrina Centro

11. PLATO DE LOS MONTES DE MALAGA

This dish is perfect for adventurers and hikers who have worked up a substantial appetite exploring the nearby mountains or the El Torcal nature reserve. Plato de los Montes de Malaga boasts a hearty combination of flavors: crispy fried potatoes (reminiscent of patatas bravas), paired with two juicy slices of cured lomo (pork loin), chorizo, and a fried green pepper, all crowned with a sunny-side-up egg. | ***Best Place to Sample***: Venta Los Montes

12. AJOBLANCO

For aficionados of chilled soups, Ajoblanco, also known as "white gazpacho," is a must-try. It begins with soaking hard, white bread overnight, then blending it with a homemade mixture of garlic, almonds, and vinegar. This blend is whipped into a creamy emulsion with water and oil, often served with melon or grapes. A refreshing choice on summer evenings, particularly when the terral (hot, northern wind) is at its fiercest. | ***Best Place to Sample***:

Arabica Case de Vinos y Comidas

13. GAZPACHO

Gazpacho is a refreshing cold soup typically made with ripe tomatoes, bell peppers, cucumbers, onions, garlic, olive oil, vinegar, and bread, all blended together until smooth. Seasonings like salt, pepper, and sometimes cumin or paprika add depth to its flavor. Served chilled, gazpacho is perfect for hot summer days and is often garnished with diced vegetables or croutons for texture. Nonetheless, numerous excellent restaurants in Malaga serve this internationally renowned Spanish specialty, each with its unique interpretation based on family recipes. Visit the city during the peak of August, and you'll find yourself sipping this cold soup straight from the glass like a true Malagueño – a daily ritual during the summer heat. | **Best Place to Sample**: Restaurante El Pantano

14. AJOBACALAO

For fans of migas who have wondered if there's a fish-based version of this rustic dish made from leftovers, behold Ajobacalao! Prepared with day-old bread crumbs, garlic, anchovies, and peppers, seasoned with paprika and lemon juice, it's a dish impossible not to savor. | **Best Place to Sample**: Tapeo de Cervantes

15. MOLLETES

Resembling pita bread, molletes are soft white rolls and a beloved breakfast staple. Typically served with olive oil and a variety of toppings, from jamon serrano or york to cheese, they're affordable, wholesome, and incredibly delicious. | **Best Place to Sample**: Restaurante Galvez

16. BOQUERONES EN VINAGRE

While Malaga boasts numerous fantastic dining spots, if you're seeking your inaugural taste of boquerones en vinagre, Marisquería la Mayor is the place to be. This modern and vibrant eatery serves up the finest anchovies marinated in vinegar – a delightful accompaniment suitable for any season. A superb lunch option in Malaga! | **Best Place to Sample**: Marisquería la Mayor

17. GAMBAS AL PIL-PIL

I must confess, I never thought I'd encounter a spot serving gambas al pil-pil as impeccably prepared as my mother-in-law's. However, during my quest to uncover the finest eateries in Malaga, Spain, I stumbled upon one contender that could give my mother-in-law a run for her money: Cortijo de Pepe. Served piping hot with a fiery kick, the gambas al pil-pil at Cortijo de Pepe are sure to leave you thoroughly satisfied. | ***Best Place to Sample***: Cortijo de Pepe

18. PASAS – SUNDRIED RAISINS

Malagueños adore their pasas, sundried raisins – whether as a snack or an ingredient in dessert specialties like Tarta Malagueña. The most coveted pasas are the authentic Moscatel raisins derived from – you guessed it – the Moscatel grape, native to the Malaga region. A visit to the renowned Atarazanas food market ranks among the top experiences in Malaga, and it's also where you'll find the finest pasas. | ***Best Place to Sample***: Mercado Central de Atarazanas

19. PIPIRRANA

Pipirrana is a straightforward salad enjoyed during spring and summer, with variations across Spain. In Malaga, it often features pulpo (octopus) or fish roe, while maintaining a base of diced onions, red peppers, and tomatoes, dressed with vinegar, salt, and olive oil. | ***Best Place to Sample***: Meson Mariano

20. ALBONDIGAS IN ALMOND SAUCE

Delicate meatballs crafted from ground beef or a blend of beef and pork, gently simmered in a luscious almond sauce steal the spotlight in this dish. The sauce, a true star, boasts a rich complexity, enhanced by toasted almonds, bread, garlic, spices, and occasionally saffron. Traditionally presented as a main course, it's often accompanied by rice, potatoes, or crusty bread to fully savor the delectable sauce. | ***Best Place to Sample***: Bar Restaurante Hermanos Rodriguez

21. BERENJENAS FRITAS CON MIEL DE CAÑA

Thin slices of eggplant are coated in locally sourced cane honey & fried to sweet perfection – a delightful appetizer to kick off your meal with these exquisitely prepared veggies. | ***Best Place to Sample***: Casa Manuel de la Lonja

22. OLIVES FROM MALAGA

As you venture through the countryside around Malaga, you'll encounter numerous fields lined with olive trees, the source of the region's finest olives and olive oil. To procure your own supply of olives for evening snacks in your holiday apartment or to take home, visit Malaga's Atarazanas food market. | ***Best Place to Sample***: Mercado Central de Atarazanas

23. CARTOJAL WINE

If you find yourself in Malaga during the feria, you'll likely be introduced to the renowned Vino Cartojal – a chilled white wine sipped from the colorful cups typical of the feria grounds. Crafted at the Malaga Virgen Bodegas near the picturesque *Fuente de la Piedra lakes*, where flamingos can be spotted at certain times of the year, this vineyard is a must-visit. | **_Best Place to Sample_**: Malaga Virgen Bodegas

24. GACHAS MALAGUEÑAS

Gachas Malagueñas is a hearty porridge crafted from flour, water, and olive oil, renowned for its thick consistency. It's commonly adorned with a delectable topping of honey, cinnamon, and raisins, making it a satisfying and nourishing dish enjoyed either for breakfast or as a hearty snack. This traditional dish suitable for breakfast or desser. | **_Best Place to Sample_**: Meson Mariano

25. PAELLA IN A BEACH BAR

Malagueño paella is renowned for its distinctive character, typically abundant in fresh seafood such as prawns, mussels, and clams, harmoniously combined with rice, vegetables, and occasionally chicken or rabbit. This traditional rice dish is prepared in a paellera, a large pan often set over a fire pit and cooked outdoors. For the ultimate paella experience in Malaga, venture to Chiringuito Litoral Pacifico, located on the street named after Malaga's own Hollywood star, Antonio Banderas. | **_Best Place to Sample_**: Chiringuito Litoral Pacifico

TOP BREAKFAST RESTAURANTS

For the best breakfast in Málaga, start your day right at one of the cafes below, where you can indulge in traditional Spanish breakfast delights: **1. Cafe Central(Plaza de la Constitución, 11, Málaga):** Begin your morning with people-watching while enjoying a steaming hot coffee of your choice, from café sombra to nube. Pair it with a pitufo, the finest Spanish bread with olive oil and your choice of jamón serrano or ibérico, tomate, or marmalade.

2. Bertani Cafe (Calle San Juan 40, Málaga): If all you need is a shot of espresso to kickstart your day, head to Bertani Café. This cozy spot excels in crafting cappuccinos and foam. Grab your coffee and small breakfast bites to go or savor them in the retro pink interior.

3. La Galerna (Paseo Marítimo el Pedregal, 66, Málaga): For a picturesque seaside breakfast experience with ocean views, visit La Galerna. Offering a variety of breads, including multigrain and gluten-free options, along with fresh juices and a diverse tea selection, La Galerna prioritizes healthy choices and good vibes.

4. Santa Coffee (C. Tomás Heredia, 5, Málaga): Whether you prefer sweet or savory breakfast options, Santa Coffee specializes in specialty coffee and homemade cakes, also selling their roasted coffee. Indulge in fresh avocado on an open sandwich with greens and tomatoes or treat yourself to homemade cookies, cakes, or pastries alongside your morning coffee, all at fair prices.

5. Mia Coffee Shop (Plaza de los Mártires, 4 Málaga): Another top spot for morning indulgence is Mia Coffee Shop, located in Plaza de los Mártires, just a short walk from the famous Museo Carmen Thyssen. Here, you'll find fresh croissants, fantastic coffee, and divine muffins and brownies – perfect for those with a sweet tooth.

TOP BRUNCH SPOTS

When it comes to finding the perfect brunch spot in Málaga, look no further than La Galerna. Historically, Andalusians stuck to a traditional breakfast at 10 AM and lunch at 2 PM, leaving little room for brunch. However, following the trend of cosmopolitan cities like Madrid and Barcelona, Málaga has embraced this mealtime evolution.

Brunchit Coffee & Kitchen – Located at Calle Carretería, 46, Málaga: Indulge in the freshest fare Málaga has to offer at Brunchit Coffee & Kitchen. Savor fluffy American-style pancakes drizzled in chocolate sauce, eggs Benedict, refreshing smoothies, and a selection of homemade bread from the in-house bakery.

Santa Canela – Found at Calle Tomás Heredia, 5, Málaga: Discover culinary creativity in Málaga's vibrant Soho district at Santa Canela. Treat yourself to Spanish crepes, artisanal cakes, nourishing smoothies, salads, and cereals amidst the district's captivating street art and eclectic shops.

Desal Cafe – Situated at Calle Nosquera 2, 29008 Málaga: For a health-conscious brunch experience in a charming setting, Desal Cafe is a must-visit. Choose from an array of cheese & jamón platters, inventive salads, and hearty sandwiches crafted to fuel your day.

Byoko – Located at Plaza de la Merced, 22, Málaga: Nestled in the bustling Plaza de la Merced, Byoko stands out as a premier brunch destination dedicated to locally sourced ingredients. Indulge in delectable bagels featuring salmon and avocado, fried goat cheese with honey, or the tantalizing "guacamozza."

Gloria Hoyos – Found at Calle Carretería 89, Local Bajo, Málaga: For a global-inspired brunch experience, head to Gloria Hoyos near the Picasso Museum. Enjoy an eclectic assortment of sandwiches, burgers, and dips, including baba ganoush and "lagrimas de cocodrilo" – chicken fried with nachos and melted cheddar cheese.

TOP LUNCH SPOTS

Lunch holds a special place in Andalusian culture, embodying leisure and social connection. To truly experience the essence of lunchtime in Málaga, embrace the local tradition of starting with shared tapas before indulging in main courses. Here are five standout restaurants to explore for lunch:

ANDINO GASTROBAR – Calle Calderón de la Barca 3, Málaga: Blend Latin American specialties with Spanish tapas at this centrally located gem. Andino Gastrobar offers a diverse menu catering to various dietary preferences, ensuring a culinary adventure worth every cent.

CASAAMIGOS – Calle Nosquera, 14 Local Izq, Málaga: Perfect for group gatherings, Casaamigos presents a modern twist on traditional dishes, served in a chic setting. Expect inventive takes on classics, like patatas bravas with a spicy foam twist.

RESTAURANTE PICASSO – Plaza de la Merced 19-20, Málaga: Named after the city's famous artist, this eatery pairs an affordable tapas deal with globally inspired meat dishes. Enjoy a leisurely meal followed by a digestif, all within proximity to Picasso's birthplace.

SIETE SEMILLAS – Plaza Arriola 1, Málaga: Located near the Guadalmedina river, Siete Semillas offers ecologically conscious cuisine featuring both meat and plant-based options. Indulge in seasonal delights crafted with care and attention to dietary needs.

KORTXO – Calle Salinas 3, Málaga: For special occasions, Kortxo impresses with its elegant ambiance and tantalizing menu. Signature dishes like cod croquettes and Russian salad with avocado mayo elevate dining experiences in Málaga.

LA RISTOBOTTEGA – Calle Cañón 3, 29015: Here traditional recipes are prepared with passion. From authentic cold cuts to comforting baked pasta, every dish offers a taste of Italy in the heart of Málaga, accompanied by top-notch service.

TOP 20 TAPAS YOU MUST TRY

Tapas, originating from Spain, are delectable small dishes that have transcended mere food to become a communal dining experience, where friends and family share an assortment of plates. Traditionally, tapas were complimentary snacks accompanying drinks, but now they're commonly priced individually. They boast a wide variety of flavors and ingredients, catering to diverse tastes and dietary needs. Whether savory or sweet, hot or cold, there's a tapa to delight every palate!

Here are some of the finest Spanish tapas you should definitely try, along with recipes straight from a local kitchen:

1. JAMÓN IBÉRICO AND CHEESE: A classic Spanish starter, the tabla de jamón Ibérico and cheese, requires minimal preparation time, making it a favorite tapa in various regions of Spain. Opt for jamón de bellota for the best flavor, as it's derived from pigs fed natural products, lending a distinctive taste to the meat. When indulging in these tapas, prioritize local products for an authentic gastronomic experience.

2. FRIED ANCHOVIES: Pescaíto frito, a beloved Andalusian appetizer, typically features fresh fish, with fried anchovies being a standout option. The secret to these delectable Spanish snacks lies in the simple flour coating, resulting in a crispy exterior and flavorful interior. While choices of fish may be limited, be sure to inquire about the best fish of the day at local restaurants.

3. BERENJENAS FRITAS CON MIEL (FRIED EGGPLANTS WITH HONEY): Berenjenas fritas con miel, a delightful tapa popular in Málaga, offers a unique flavor experience. Thin slices of eggplant are coated in flour, fried to perfection, and then drizzled with locally sourced honey, renowned for its natural and distinctive taste. For an original tapas idea, don't miss out on this flavorful dish.

4. CAZON EN ADOBO (MARINATED CAZON FISH): Hailing from the Cadiz region of southern Andalucía, Cazon en Adobo showcases the abundance of white fish in the area. Marinated with garlic, sweet pepper, cumin, and oregano, the fish pieces are then coated in breadcrumbs and fried to create a mouthwatering tapa that captures the essence of Spanish cuisine.

5.TORTILLA DE PATATAS (SPANISH POTATO OMELETTE): A quintessential

Spanish tapa, the famous tortilla de patatas is enjoyed throughout the country, either hot or cold. This versatile dish allows for personalization, as you can add your favorite ingredients to the mixture of eggs and potatoes. Whether you're in Andalucia during winter or summer, be sure to savor the timeless appeal of tortilla de patatas, available even in supermarkets with or without onions.

6. ALBÓNDIGAS (SPANISH MEATBALLS): Albóndigas offer a versatile tapas experience, as they can be prepared in various ways using different meats & sauces. The traditional recipe typically features pork seasoned with pepper, garlic, and parsley, with optional additions of eggs & breadcrumbs for a firmer texture. Serve these delectable meatballs with homemade tomato sauce to elevate their flavor.

7. SPANISH CHICKEN CROQUETTES: Croquetas rank among the most beloved traditional Spanish tapas, with Spanish ham croquettes being a popular choice. For a lighter alternative, consider taking chicken croquettes. These tapas pair perfectly with Spanish wines and are made by combining boiled chicken meat and milk to achieve a creamy consistency. Shape the mixture into croquettes, coat them in breadcrumbs, and fry until golden brown.

8. SPANISH DEVILED EGGS (HUEVOS RELLENOS): Spanish deviled eggs are a flavorful starter with countless variations, offering options for both vegetarians and meat lovers. A popular rendition includes filling boiled egg whites with a mixture of tuna and tomato sauce, garnished with sweet Spanish paprika or mayonnaise. Ensure these tasty tapas remain refrigerated to preserve their flavor.

9. SPANISH CHORIZO RECIPE WITH CIDER (CHORIZO A LA SIDRA): Chorizo a la sidra is a beloved Spanish dish, especially during autumn when apples are ripe and flavorful. This simple recipe involves cooking chorizo in apple cider, resulting in a sizzling and savory tapa that's perfect for a Spanish-themed party. Saute garlic in a clay pot, add cider and bay leaves, bring to a boil, then add chorizo chunks and simmer for 30 minutes until sizzling.

10. SPANISH STUFFED PEPPERS: Piquillo stuffed peppers are a cherished tapa from Andalucía, although their unique taste may not appeal to all palates. To prepare them at home, acquire canned piquillo peppers and fill them with a mixture of bechamel and tomato sauce, optionally adding canned tuna or diced cured ham. Serve these flavorful stuffed peppers cold or warm to suit your preference.

11. FRIED FLAMENQUINES CORDOBESES: Flamenquines cordobeses rank among the finest Spanish tapas in Andalucía, celebrated for their simplicity and exquisite flavor. These delightful treats are crafted by stuffing pork loin steaks with ham and cheese, rolling them up, coating them in breadcrumbs, and frying until golden brown. To avoid any mess, ensure the cheese is at room temperature before assembling. Enjoy these crispy delights with ease!

12. BACALAO CROQUETTES: Spanish croquettes are beloved nationwide, with certain types gaining popularity based on regional preferences. Bacalao croquettes, featuring cod, are particularly favored in coastal regions of Spain. While not overly complex, their preparation is time-consuming. Boil cod and potatoes, then mix and shape the dough into croquettes. Coat them in egg, flour, and breadcrumbs before frying. Serve these flavorful croquettes hot or cold for a delightful tapas experience.

13. BEEF EMPANADAS: Spanish empanadas are a convenient snack for exploring cities without stopping for a full meal. Available in various fillings, including chicken, lamb, beef, or squid, these savory turnovers consist of a dough stuffed with cooked ground meat, peas, onion, and olive oil, baked to perfection. Ideal for on-the-go snacking, empanadas offer a satisfying taste of Spanish cuisine.

14. FRIED BABY SQUID (PUNTILLITAS FRITAS): Fried baby squid is a delightful Spanish appetizer, boasting a crunchy exterior and tender interior. Simply coat baby squids in flour and fry until golden brown for a finger-licking tapas experience. Garnish with a squeeze of lemon juice for added zest and enjoy this easy-to-make delicacy that's sure to impress your guests.

15. BOQUERONES EN VINAGRE (ANCHOVIES IN VINEGAR): Boquerones en vinagre are a beloved Spanish tapa, perfect for pairing with cold beers. Marinate fresh anchovies in vinegar, garlic, and parsley for at least 24 hours in the refrigerator to infuse them with bold flavors. The simplicity of preparation ensures that these tangy treats are quick and easy to enjoy, with the quality of ingredients enhancing their overall taste.

16. PATATAS BRAVAS: Patatas bravas, a classic Spanish dish, is perfect for sharing with friends over a few beers. Potatoes are typically cut into large cubes, fried until crispy, and served with a spicy sauce. The sauce features garlic, sweet and spicy ground peppers, chicken broth, and flour, creating a simple yet delicious accompaniment to the crispy potatoes.

17. GAMBAS AL PIL PIL (GARLIC PRAWNS IN SPICY OIL): Gambas al pil pil, also known as gambas al ajillo, are Spain's renowned tapas, often served sizzling in restaurants. Made with prawns, olive oil, garlic, and spices, this dish relies on quality ingredients for its bold flavors. Quick and easy to prepare, gambas al pil pil is a delightful option for any tapas spread.

18. BREAD WITH TOMATO (PAN CON TOMATE): Pan con tomate is a popular Spanish appetizer consisting of toasted bread topped with garlic and a chunky tomato spread. With only bread and tomato as essential ingredients, this dish offers flexibility for substitutions and variations. A simple yet flavorful tapas option, pan con tomate is easily prepared using basic kitchen tools.

19. BLACK PUDDING (MORCILLA): Black pudding, also known as morcilla in Spain, adds rich flavor to traditional stews and dishes. Made from blood and sometimes boiled rice, its distinctive taste may not appeal to everyone. Often found in hot stews, black pudding enhances the depth of flavor in various Spanish recipes.

20. ENSALADA RUSA (RUSSIAN SALAD): Ensalada rusa, or Russian salad, reigns as one of Spain's favorite tapas, cherished for its simplicity and nutritional value. Boiled potatoes, carrots, eggs, and green beans are cubed and mixed with mayonnaise, with optional additions of canned tuna. Chilled before serving, this refreshing salad is a delightful addition to any tapas spread.

TOP 5 TAPAS SPOTS

Regardless of your location in Andalusia, indulging in tapas in Málaga should be a priority. Dining, whether savoring tapas or enjoying a standard meal, is a communal affair here, sparking joy and lively conversation as you share an array of delectable tapas with loved ones. Places to Indulge in Tapas in Malaga include:

LAS NIÑAS DEL SOHO – LOCATED AT CALLE SAN LORENZO 27, MÁLAGA: Following a morning spent exploring the latest exhibitions at the Centro de Arte Contemporàneo (CAC), a brief stroll brings you to one of Málaga's trendiest tapas bars – Las Niñas del Soho. Renowned for its eclectic mix of traditional tapas with inventive twists and fusions, this establishment has earned a special place in the hearts of locals.

EL TAPEO DE CERVANTES – FOUND AT CALLE CÀRCER 8, MÁLAGA: A stone's throw from the historic Teatro Cervantes, El Tapeo de Cervantes awaits, offering one of the premier tapas experiences in Málaga before attending a performance. From classic dishes like porra Antequerana to innovative creations like grilled bluefin tuna with cauliflower emulsion, the menu promises a culinary adventure. Don't miss their selection of sweet wines!

CASA LOLA – LOCATED AT CALLE GRANADA 46, 29015, WITH TWO ADDITIONAL LOCATIONS IN THE CITY: Casa Lola prides itself on using the finest Spanish ingredients, resulting in dishes bursting with freshness and flavor. Indulge in their Basque-inspired pinchos or sample their legendary patatas bravas. Nestled on the pedestrian-friendly Calle Granada, this venue provides the ideal backdrop for enjoying tapas paired with their renowned vermouth. Despite its expansion to three locations, the original establishment on Calle Granada remains a beloved choice for many.

LA TRANCA – SITUATED AT CALLE CARRETERÍA 92, MÁLAGA: This tapas bar not only entices with its exceptional menu but also boasts exquisite decor, making it one of the premier dining destinations in Malaga city. Adorned with vintage photographs of Spain's and Andalucia's luminaries, including revered bullfighters and musical icons, La Tranca offers a feast for the eyes as well as the palate.

BODEGUITA EL GALLO – FOUND AT CALLE SAN AGUSTÍN 19, MÁLAGA:

For an authentic tapas experience in the heart of Málaga's old town, look no further than Bodeguita el Gallo, just around the corner from the Museo Picasso. This family-owned establishment serves up traditional tapas in small, medium, or full portions, always accompanied by warm hospitality. When pondering where to dine in Malaga's old town during your visit, Bodeguita el Gallo stands out as the ideal choice.

AUTHENTIC SEAFOOD JOINTS

Given Malaga's coastal location, the abundance of seafood options is undeniable, prompting the need to distinguish between seafood restaurants and "chiringuitos" (beach bars). While both offer seafood and various fish dishes, chiringuitos specialize in fried fish, paellas, and skewered specialties like the renowned "espetos" (sardines). Their peak season is typically summer when beachside locations draw maximum crowds. The focus of this section is to highlight the top seafood restaurants in Malaga, where you can indulge in the finest fresh produce, complemented by meticulously curated wine selections. Below are the top five seafood restaurants in Malaga, where you can savor authentic seafood dishes that will surely leave you coming back for more.

1. LOS MARINOS JOSÉ: Renowned as the best seafood restaurant in Malaga, Los Marinos José has garnered accolades such as two stars from the Repsol Guide and the 'ABC' chili sauce prize. It has also been listed in the "Top Ten" in the Tradition and Product category of the OAD list. The restaurant's success lies in its commitment to fresh, top-quality ingredients, many of which are caught daily. The menu is crafted each morning based on the available products. Moreover, Los Marinos José offers creative dishes like the anchovy roe omelette and morrillo mojama, alongside an extensive wine list featuring over 250 national and international selections. | **Location:** Sea Walk Rey de España, 161, 29640 Fuengirola (Malaga)

2. DORAMAR: Doramar is a classic seafood destination in Malaga, serving high-quality seafood for nearly three decades. With two locations in the Ciudad Jardin district & the center of Malaga (Soho), Doramar is renowned for its exceptional service and top-notch products. The menu boasts a wide selection, including oysters, coquinas, lobster, and other delicacies such as spider crab & red tuna of Almadraba. Additionally, Doramar Puerto offers an array of grilled meat options alongside its seafood menu, complemented by an impressive wine selection featuring over 140 labels. | *Locations:* Emilio Díaz Street, 46, 29014 Málaga; | Casas de Campos Street, 1, 29001 Málaga

3. DEHUELVA: DeHuelva distinguishes itself by sourcing all its products from the province of Huelva, renowned for its quality seafood. Located in the Huelin neighborhood, DeHuelva offers a diverse menu featuring fish, seafood, paellas, and regional specialties such as tiger prawns and mojama of Isla Cristina. The restaurant's star product is the white prawns of Huelva. Despite a modest wine selection, the quality and value of the offerings are noteworthy. | **Location:** Antonio Soler Street, 5, local 3, 29002 Malaga

4. EL CATETO: El Cateto, originally a breakfast cafeteria over 30 years ago, has evolved into a premier seafood destination in Malaga. Combining tradition with innovation, El Cateto offers a menu rich in traditional cuisine alongside fresh seafood sourced from the Caleta de Velez market. Signature dishes include oysters, pebbles, thin shells, and grilled Garrucha prawns. The restaurant also features stews and other traditional fare, attracting athletes and renowned chefs alike. | **Location:** Pedro de Lobo Street, 3, 29014 Malaga

5. LOS MELLIZOS: Los Mellizos is a prominent restaurant group with eight locations across the province of Malaga. Each establishment offers a varied menu comprising fish, seafood, fried delicacies, rice dishes, and meat specialties. While the menu is consistent across all locations, each restaurant has its own specialties tailored to different preferences and budgets. Options include paellas, fried pescaíto (small fried fish), espetos (skewered fish), seafood, and tapas, with group menus also available. | **Location:** Multiple locations including Benalmádena, Málaga, and Marbella

TOP BAR TO HAVE A DRINK LIKE A LOCAL

Discovering Malaga's vibrant nightlife scene is an essential part of experiencing the city like a local. From sunny terraces to lively bars, Malaga offers a plethora of options for enjoying drinks and tapas with friends. Here are some of the best bars in Malaga that are favored by the locals: **1. EL ALMACÉN DEL INDIANO:** This neighborhood bar exudes charm and tradition, reminiscent of Malaga's past. Serving authentic homemade cuisine and local wines in a setting that recalls old ultramarinos shops, El Almacén del Indiano is a perfect spot for a relaxed drink and conversation. | **2. CENTRAL BEERS:** For beer enthusiasts, Central Beers is a must-visit. This modern gastro pub and craft beer bar boasts an extensive selection of craft beers from around the world, paired with delicious pub snacks. Whether you're unwinding during the day or seeking a lively atmosphere at night, Central Beers offers a diverse and exciting drinking experience. | **3. LA TRANCA:** Paying homage to Malaga's culture and history, La Tranca is adorned with album covers and photos of famous Spanish musicians. This bustling hangout is popular among locals for its selection of wines, vermouth, and local beers, served alongside classic tapas like ensaladilla and tortilla. | **4. MESON ANTONIO**: With over 30 years of history, Meson Antonio is a beloved bar known for its lively atmosphere, unbeatable tapas, and extensive wine list. Wine lovers will appreciate the selection of local wines, while the traditional decoration and ambiance add to the charm of this Malaga favorite. | **5. ROOM MATE LARIOS ROOFTOP TERRACE:** For stunning views of Malaga, head to the rooftop terrace of the Room Mate Larios Hotel. Offering panoramic views of the city center, this rooftop bar is perfect for enjoying cocktails, local beers, and wine while soaking in the breathtaking scenery.

6 BEST PLACES TO ENJOY WINE

Exploring Malaga's gastronomic scene isn't complete without sampling its excellent local wines. Here are six perfect places in Malaga where you can enjoy a glass or two of the finest vino after a day of sightseeing or biking: **1. EL PIMPI:** A true institution in Malaga, El Pimpi offers an authentic bodega experience in a charming 18th-century mansion. With its labyrinthine layout featuring quaint patios and rooms adorned with memorabilia, El Pimpi is the perfect spot to savor local wines while taking in views of the Alcazaba and Roman Theatre. | **2. LA ANTIGUA CASA DE GUARDIA:** As one of the oldest establishments in the city, La Antigua Casa de Guardia transports visitors back in time with its traditional ambiance and selection of wines served straight from giant barrels. Enjoy cold tapas like prawns and cheese alongside your wine in this historic setting. | **3. LA ODISEA:** Nestled in the Alcazaba hillside, La Odisea offers a unique wine-drinking experience in an 18th-century house with cave-like back rooms. Enjoy local wines on the small outside terrace overlooking Paseo del Parque, or sample homemade vermouth and tapas in the cozy interior. | **4. ANYWAY WINE BAR:** Located in La Malagueta, Anyway Wine Bar is known for its fine wines and dining experience. Pair plates of cheese and Iberian cold cuts with expertly selected wines recommended by the staff. | **5. LOS PATIOS DE BEATAS:** With over 600 wine labels to choose from, Los Patios de Beatas is a haven for wine enthusiasts. Enjoy a wide selection of wines by the glass and creative tapas in the stunning 18th and 19th-century patios. | **6. VINO MIO:** Run by a Dutch team next to the Cervantes Theatre, Vino Mio boasts an impressive wine list and offers High Wine tastings where you can sample three different wines paired with tapas. Perfect for a late-afternoon indulgence after a day of biking or beach exploration.

THE BEST FOOD MARKETS

Exploring the vibrant markets of Malaga offers a delightful journey into the heart of the city's culture and culinary traditions. Here are some of the best markets you should definitely visit:

1. MERCADO CENTRAL DE ATARAZANAS: Located at Calle Atarazanas, 10, the Atarazanas market is a must-visit destination for both locals and tourists. Originally a shipyard during Muslim times, this market now offers a diverse array of food items, including fresh seafood, meats, fruits, and vegetables. Don't miss the opportunity to enjoy some of the best tapas in the city while you're here.

2. MERCADO DE SALAMANCA: Situated at Calle San Bartolomé, 1, the Mercado de Salamanca may not be as well-known among tourists, but it's highly popular among locals. Built in a neo-Arabic style between 1922 and 1925, this market boasts a charming atmosphere and a wide selection of fresh produce and local delicacies.

3. MERCADO EL CARMEN: If you're a seafood lover, don't miss Mercado el Carmen at Calle la Serna, 3. This market, located in the El Perchel neighborhood, has been serving the community for over 140 years and is renowned for its quality fish and seafood. You'll also find a variety of meats, vegetables, and other fresh products here.

4. GUADALHORCE ORGANIC MARKET: For those interested in organic produce, the Guadalhorce Organic Market is a must-visit. Held twice a month at different locations, this open-air market offers a wide range of organic fruits, vegetables, spices, and more. Check their schedule for the nearest location to you.

5. CORTIJO DE TORRES FLEA MARKET: For a unique shopping experience, head to the Cortijo de Torres Flea Market, located next to Recinto Ferial. Open every Sunday from 10:00 to 15:00, this market offers everything from clothing and jewelry to antiques and furniture. Don't forget to explore the food and produce section while you're there.

6. MADE IN SOHO MARKET: Experience the creativity of local artisans at the Made in Soho Market, held on the first Saturday of every month at Calle Tomás de Heredia. This open-air market showcases a variety of art, crafts, clothing, and local products, providing the perfect opportunity to support local craftsmanship and find unique souvenirs.

7. MONTHLY FARMERS MARKETS: The monthly farmers market organized by the 'Guadalhorce Ecologico Cooperativa' brings the freshest and most eco-friendly produce from Malaga's Guadalhorce Valley to the city. This initiative, which started about seven years ago, tours Malaga province every second and fourth Saturday of the month. You can find the market set up on Calle Cervantes, near the historic bullring, where colorful open-air stalls offer a wide range of organic products, from fruits and vegetables to chocolate and pasta.

8. MERCADO DE LA MERCED: Mercado de la Merced, located near Plaza Merced in Malaga's old town, underwent a significant renovation and reopened in October 2015. It's not just a place to shop for food anymore; it has become one of the trendiest spots for dining and drinking in the city. With 22 stalls offering a variety of goods, including cured meats, fresh seafood, vegetables, and even designer tapas bars and sushi stalls, Mercado de la Merced is a hub of culinary innovation and excellence. It's a blend of the traditional Andalusian market experience with modern international influences, making it a must-visit destination for food enthusiasts in Malaga.

Whether you're in search of fresh ingredients, unique gifts, or simply want to immerse yourself in the lively atmosphere of Malaga's markets, these destinations offer something for everyone to enjoy.

TOP 5 MALAGA CUISINE COOKING CLASSES

If you're eager to recreate the flavors of Spanish cuisine at home, the 5 recommended cooking classes in Malaga below offer the perfect opportunity to learn from local experts and dive into the culinary traditions of the region.

1. A COOKING DAY: Located in a picturesque farmhouse in the countryside near Malaga, A Cooking Day offers authentic cooking experiences rooted in traditional recipes passed down through generations. With a focus on using fresh, seasonal ingredients, owner Mayte welcomes guests into her family's home to learn the secrets behind beloved Spanish dishes. | **Website:** https://www.acookingday.com

2. LA ROSILLA: Escape the city and immerse yourself in rural Spain with La Rosilla's Cooking & Culture Days. Set in a beautiful country home, these classes provide a hands-on experience in preparing simple and delicious Spanish cuisine, surrounded by stunning mountain views and the tranquility of the countryside. | **Website:** https://larosilla-catering.com

3. ANDALUCÍA EXPERIENCIAS' ESPETO WORKSHOP ON THE BEACH: Experience Malaga's coastal charm with Andalucía Experiencias' espeto workshop, where you'll learn to grill the perfect salty sardines right on the beach. Explore a traditional fishermen's quarter, visit a maritime museum, and master the art of making espetos before enjoying a beachfront dining experience. | **Website:** https://www.andaluciaexperiencias.com/en/taller-de-espetos-malaga

4. SPAIN FOOD SHERPAS: Dive into Malaga's vibrant food scene with Spain Food Sherpas' tapas and paella cooking classes. Begin with a visit to Atarazanas Market to source fresh ingredients before heading to the kitchen to prepare regional specialties. Wine and olive oil tastings enhance the culinary experience. | **Website:** https://www.spainfoodsherpas.com

5. AIL MALAGA SPANISH & COOKING CLASSES: Combine language learning with culinary exploration at AIL Malaga's Spanish & Cooking Classes. Perfect for those staying longer in Malaga, these courses offer a unique blend of Spanish lessons and hands-on cooking sessions, allowing you to master both the language and cuisine of Spain. | **Website:** *https://www.ailmalaga.com/spanish-cooking-malaga*

Whether you're a novice cook or a seasoned foodie, these cooking classes offer an immersive and educational experience that will deepen your appreciation for Spanish gastronomy. Don't miss out on the opportunity to learn from local experts and bring the flavors of Malaga into your own kitchen!

10 HIDDEN GEM RESTAURANTS

1. MAMUCHIS

Mamuchis, located in the trendy Soho area of Málaga, proudly boasts the slogan "Healthy foods of the world." This charming bistro offers a unique menu of sharing dishes influenced by Mediterranean, Asian, and Latin American cuisines. The idea is to order a diverse selection from the menu and enjoy a culinary journey around the world with friends. The restaurant's fancy and old-school interior, featuring upcycled furniture, creates a distinctive atmosphere. Mamuchis is easily recognizable from a distance, adorned with a vibrant and sizable painting on the exterior. Additionally, there is a small terrace where you can dine outdoors while indulging in a bit of people-watching.

2. FONZO TAPAS BAR

Fonzo Tapas Bar is an absolute must-visit when you're in Málaga! This trendy and vibrant tapas bar is a hidden gem. The menu features delicious and highly creative vegetarian dishes, as well as options with meat. The entire kitchen revolves around fresh vegetables, herbs, and flavorful spices, with a focus on local, seasonal, and organic ingredients. Due to this commitment, the menu changes periodically. Fonzo's motto is "real food tastes best," and this philosophy is evident in every tapas plate they serve. A visit to Fonzo promises an evening filled with soulful food and great drinks, creating memories to cherish.

3. LA RECOVA

For those who appreciate more traditional fare, La Recova is a must-try for breakfast or tapas. Seating tends to fill up rapidly, both outdoors and indoors, so consider avoiding peak times. What's on the menu? A substantial thick slice of toasted bread accompanied by an array of homemade spreads, including two different meat mousses, mousse with peppers and dried tomatoes, delightful jams, slices of tomatoes, and some fruit. La Recova is a true hidden gem, tucked away at the back of an antique shop.

4. LOVA CAFÉ

This cafe is our absolute favorite in Málaga for every occasion – be it breakfast, lunch, dinner, or just a quick stop for coffee and cake. They prioritize using local and organic products for their dishes whenever possible, catering to vegetarians and vegans as well. On Sundays, you can also reserve a brunch for €15.90. In the evening, the menu undergoes a slight change, offering delightful Japanese cuisine. The stunning interior, adorned with fancy wallpaper, Bali-style lamps, and cozy chairs, creates an inviting ambiance that makes you want to linger all day long.

5. BAR MOLINILLO 33 – SECRET BAR WITH THE BEST SPANISH & ARGENTINIAN FOOD

Bar Molinillo 33 is a hidden gem in the heart of Malaga, offering a delightful culinary experience with a fusion of Spanish and Argentinian flavors. Tucked away from the main tourist areas, this secret bar, located near Mercado de Salamanca, is a local favorite known for its exceptional Andalusian cuisine, warm hospitality, and reasonable prices. Despite being in the historic center, Bar Molinillo 33 remains a well-kept secret, making it an ideal spot for those seeking an authentic local experience. The cozy establishment has gained popularity among locals for its traditional Andalusian dishes and an extensive selection of drinks, all at a fraction of the cost compared to more touristy restaurants on Granada street. Due to its small size, the bar tends to fill up quickly, especially on Fridays and Saturdays, so arriving early is advisable. Visitors can enjoy a laid-back atmosphere, engage in friendly conversations, and relish the diverse menu featuring Mexican, Argentinian, and Andalusian delights. Signature dishes include empanadas, patatas fritas, bondiola de cerdo, croquetas, and, of course, mouthwatering tacos. Complement your meal with a glass of their delicious red wine or locally produced Malaga beer. Bar Molinillo 33 provides a genuine taste of local life, making it a perfect choice for those looking to immerse themselves in the authentic culinary scene of Malaga.

6. DESAL CAFE – LESSER-KNOWN BREAKFAST SPOT IN MALAGA

Desal Cafe stands out as one of Malaga's hidden breakfast gems, offering a delightful and budget-friendly morning experience with stunning views. With two somewhat concealed locations in the city center, Desal Cafe provides a perfect blend of delicious breakfast options, a variety of food choices, and reasonable prices. The first location, tucked away in a quiet passageway with outside tables, boasts incredible combo plates and a relaxed atmosphere. Desal Cafe's commitment to affordability is evident, offering breakfast options for as little as €5, which includes a meal and a hot drink. The inviting interior and pleasant ambiance make it a standout choice. The second location, situated on a side street, maintains the same menu and breakfast options. Noteworthy are their scrumptious benedict eggs, a particular favorite. Despite being slightly off the beaten path, this location offers a unique charm and a chance to enjoy breakfast with a view of the Parroquia de los Santos Mártires Ciriaco y Paula church. The outdoor tables near the entrance facing the church provide a peaceful setting, often occupied but accessible to those arriving early when the cafe opens. Desal Cafe captures the essence of a hidden culinary gem, offering a delightful start to the day for locals and visitors alike.

7. O MELHOR CROISSANT - UNIQUE CROISSANT PLACE

Despite being located in the most touristy part of Malaga, right in front of the famous Mercado Central, O Melhor Croissant manages to stay under the radar as visitors often flock to the market for seafood and paella, missing out on hidden culinary gems around. What sets O Melhor Croissant apart is its unconventional take on croissants. The dough, slightly sweet with a caramelized top and sugar powder, creates a unique canvas for both savory and sweet fillings. For those open to new flavor experiences, the savory croissants with tangy salads, tuna, cheese, or Iberian ham are a must-try. Seating near the window allows patrons to enjoy their croissants while observing the lively street outside. This Malaga gem offers reasonable prices and is an excellent choice for breakfast, brunch, or any time of the day, providing a distinctive twist to a classic pastry.

8. LA CATRINA CERVECERIA Y MEXICAN TAPAS

For the best Mexican food in Malaga, look no further than La Catrina Cerveceria, nestled among local bars on Juan de Padilla street. Having sampled Mexican cuisine across various Malaga restaurants, La Catrina Cerveceria stands out with its delectable nachos, burritos, enchiladas, and tacos (in competition with Bar Molinillo 33). The menu caters to various dietary preferences, offering vegetarian and gluten-free options. What makes La Catrina Cerveceria truly special is its unique and vibrant atmosphere that seamlessly blends Mexican culture with Spanish hospitality. Run by a Mexican family who moved to Spain, the restaurant boasts colorful decor,

Mexican music, and a menu that authentically captures the flavors of Mexico. A highlight is the extensive selection of craft beers, featuring both local and Mexican varieties. The bar also serves an array of tequilas and mezcals, making it a popular spot for drinks and nightlife. Despite its central location amid tourist attractions, La Catrina Cerveceria remains a hidden gem in Malaga, offering an authentic Mexican culinary experience.

9. PACO JOSE FREIDURIA DE PATATAS Y FRUTOS SECOS

Paco Jose Freiduria De Patatas y Frutos Secos is a personal favorite among the hidden gems in Malaga, especially when the craving for Spanish snacks strikes. Located in the old center of Malaga, this small snack shop, and one of the largest among its few locations, specializes in fried snacks such as patatas fritas (chips) and dried fruits and nuts. The shop also offers local candies, crystallized pineapple, sweets, souvenirs, and even beer. A must-try at Paco Jose is their traditional Malaga roasted salty almonds, providing a unique flavor experience. The shop also offers a variety of other treats, including dry apple pieces, berries, and more. Many bars and hotels in the region order nuts and chips from Paco Jose to serve with beer. Freidurias, like Paco Jose, are popular snack shops in various regions of Spain, offering quick and affordable options for both locals and visitors. Paco Jose stands out for its commitment to high-quality snacks at reasonable prices.

10. MAMA MIA ITALIAN RESTAURANT

Mama Mia, an Italian restaurant in Malaga, came highly recommended by local friends who have been residing in the city for an extended period. Specializing in Italian cuisine, particularly pizza and pasta dishes, Mama Mia has been serving locals since 1972. Despite its name, tourists rarely venture to this hidden gem. Mark and I tried gnocchi, lasagna, and maccheroni al forno, and the flavors exceeded expectations, nearly leaving our plates clean. The restaurant is praised not only for its flavorful pizzas and salads but also for its budget-friendly prices. Located away from the typical tourist areas, Mama Mia offers a cozy and relaxed atmosphere with both indoor and outdoor seating. For those seeking delicious Italian food in a local environment with reasonable prices, Mama Mia is a must-visit. The extensive menu ensures plenty of options, making it a delightful spot for a satisfying Italian meal in Malaga.

NICHOLAS INGRAM

CHAPTER 5: VIBRANT FESTIVALS & CULTURAL EVENTS

Malaga is renowned for its multitude of festivals and events held throughout the year. These celebrations range from local harvest festivals to national fiestas, each embraced with equal enthusiasm by the people of Malaga. The city and its surrounding areas host a plethora of cultural festivities, featuring lively parades, colorful events, and live music performances.

STREET FESTIVALS IN MÁLAGA

PROCESSION OF THE KINGS (PROCESIÓN DE LOS REYES): occurs on January 5th and 6th, to mark the Spanish Epiphany with a grand parade led by the three kings through the City Centre to Ayuntamiento, accompanied by heartfelt requests from children for gifts. Following the procession, the festivities continue with live music, singing, and dancing until late into the evening.

MALAGA CARNIVAL (CARNAVAL DE MÁLAGA): is a major event in Spain celebrated before the solemn period of Lent. This vibrant carnival showcases a mix of colorful costumes, multicultural performances, and street bands known as 'murgas'. The carnival procession culminates in the symbolic "burial of the sardine" at La Malagueta beach, signaling the end of the festivities. | **Date:** 3rd - 11th February 2024 | **Location:** starting from Historic Quarter

EASTER (SEMANA SANTA): stands out as a globally recognized celebration of art, devotion, and pageantry during Easter. With 42 brotherhoods parading wooden sculptures and images of the Virgin Mary through the streets, adorned in hooded robes, this event attracts visitors from around the world to witness its spectacle.

ALL SAINTS' DAY & HALLOWEEN (DIA DE TODOS LOS SANTOS): On All Saints' Day and Halloween, Spaniards commemorate their departed loved ones with visits to cemeteries, offering flowers and prayers. Meanwhile, Halloween festivities include pumpkin carving, themed parties, and children dressing up in spooky costumes.

THE NIGHT OF SAN JUAN (NOCHE DE SAN JUAN): Saint John's eve is a highly anticipated event in Malaga, drawing numerous residents and tourists to the city's beaches on the night of June 23rd to 24th each year. This festival primarily marks the celebration of the summer solstice. Thus, it serves as a festive welcome to summer, marked by various celebrations during the shortest night of the year. This tradition extends beyond Malaga, encompassing numerous regions across Spain and even other countries worldwide.

MALAGA FAIR (FERIA DE AGOSTO): In August, the Feria de Agosto, or Malaga Fair, spans nine days filled with street decorations, traditional flamenco dancing, and bullfighting at La Malagueta. | **Date:** 12th August -

19th August 2023 | **Location:** day activities at Historica Quarter and night activities at Torres district

ANDALUCIA DAY (DÍA DE ANDALUCÍA): Andalusia Day, celebrated on February 28th, commemorates the region's autonomy with flag displays and cultural competitions, often accompanied by traditional Andalusian breakfasts consisting of toast with olive oil and orange juice.

CHRISTMAS IN MALAGA: Christmas in Malaga is a magical time, especially with the enchanting illumination of Larios Street, a spectacle that never fails to captivate visitors. From late November to early January, the city is adorned with Christmas lights, filling the air with the aroma of sweets and bustling with stalls selling festive decorations. In recent years, Malaga has gained recognition as one of Europe's most charming cities during the holiday season.

THE VIRGIN OF CARMEN FESTIVITIES IN MALAGA: celebrated on July 16th, honor the patron saint of sailors and fishermen. Coastal municipalities like El Palo, Huelin, Pedregalejo, and Torremolinos participate in solemn and devout ceremonies, reflecting their deep-rooted fishing traditions. The event features a procession of the Virgin from her altar to the beach, followed by her offshore journey aboard a traditional fishing boat, the jábega. Surrounded by flowers and accompanied by a procession of city boats, worshippers seek the Virgin's protection for the city and those at sea. It's an amazing event worth experiencing firsthand.

CULTURAL EVENTS IN MÁLAGA

MÁLAGA FILM FESTIVAL: For over two decades, the Málaga Film Festival has been a proud showcase of Spanish and Latin American cinema. With premieres, award ceremonies, workshops, and documentary screenings, it honors notable figures in the film industry. While the films are primarily in Spanish and typically lack subtitles, the festival offers an excellent opportunity to immerse oneself in the language. | **Date:** March 1st - March 10th, 2024 | **Venue:** Various cinemas (Cervantes, Echegaray, and Cine Albéniz) | **MÁLAGA FLAMENCO FESTIVAL:** The Málaga Flamenco Festival presents captivating flamenco performances by top dancers and singers from Spain. Alongside mesmerizing dance shows, skilled guitarists provide musical accompaniment, offering an unforgettable experience. | **Date:** April 29th - May 27th, 2023 (biennial) | **Location:** Calle Alcazabilla | **LA NOCHE EN BLANCO MÁLAGA:** La Noche en Blanco Málaga is a highlight for culture and art enthusiasts. From 8 p.m. to midnight, many museums and galleries in Málaga open their doors to the public for free. Visitors can explore renowned institutions like the Picasso Museum and Carmen Thyssen Museum or enjoy tours at Museo Revello de Toro. The streets come alive with street art, theater, dance performances, and music, transforming Málaga into an open-air cultural hub. | **Date:** May 20th, 2023 | **MÁLAGA GASTRONOMY FESTIVAL:** Celebrating Málaga's renowned cuisine and hospitality, the Málaga Gastronomy Festival offers an immersive culinary experience. Renowned chefs from the Andalusia region showcase their skills through cooking shows and tastings, giving attendees the chance to learn and interact. Plaza de la Marina hosts the festivities, featuring food trucks and stalls offering delectable traditional Andalusian dishes such as gazpachuelo, tapas, and pipirrana salad. | **Date:** June 9th | **Location:** Plaza de la Marina

MUSIC FESTIVALS IN & AROUND MÁLAGA

The Costa del Sol is renowned for its music festivals, drawing crowds during the summer months with its mild climate, sea breeze, and spectacular stages. With excellent infrastructure and proximity to Malaga International Airport, the region offers a perfect setting for music enthusiasts. Here's a glimpse of the music festivals lined up for 2024:

LOS ÁLAMOS BEACH FESTIVAL: Málaga's stunning beaches set the stage for Andalusia's premier summer dance and electronic music festival, the Los Álamos Beach Festival. With over 40,000 attendees, this event has become a must for dance and party enthusiasts since its inception in 2015. Past line-ups have featured acclaimed artists like Fangoria, Karol G, and Oliver Heldens, accompanied by breathtaking light shows, impressive stage productions, and lively fairground attractions. | **Location:** Los Álamos Beach | **Tickets:** Day ticket €47, Day ticket with camping accommodation €67

WEEKEND BEACH FESTIVAL: The Weekend Beach Festival stands out as one of Spain's most diverse music festivals, offering a wide range of genres including house, techno, reggae, hip-hop, rock, indie, and pop. With performances by renowned artists such as Bastille, Residente, Maluma, and Nicky Jam, it promises an unforgettable musical experience. | **Location:** Torre del Mar | **Tickets:** Day ticket €49, Day ticket with camping accommodation €89

FESTIVAL INTERNACIONAL DE MÚSICA Y DANZA CUEVA DE NERJA: For over six decades, the Málaga Symphonic Orchestra has curated classical music and dance performances in the awe-inspiring setting of the Nerja Cave. This unique venue, transformed from a natural rock cave into an auditorium, offers audiences a truly extraordinary experience, combining magnificent classical performances with the unparalleled ambiance of the cave. | Date: June 30th - August 12th, 2023 | Location: Caves of Nerja | Tickets: Day tickets range from €66 to €213 | **MARENOSTRUM FUENGIROLA CONCERTS:** The Marenostrum Festival, established in 2016, has become one of the coast's premier events, featuring top artists against the backdrop of the Arab fortress Sohail, near the seafront. Past performers include Jennifer Lopez, Ricky Martin, Bob Dylan, and Sting. | **Dates:** May to September | **STARLITE MARBELLA:** Starlite Marbella is a boutique festival held in the Cantera de

Nagüeles, offering an intimate setting amidst stunning scenery. With over 50 days of concerts, the festival showcases artists like Jamie Cullum, Sheryl Crow & Aitana. | **Dates**: July to Sept. | **NERJA CAVE MUSIC FESTIVAL:** Set in the vast underground galleries of Nerja Cave, this festival features classical music and dance performances throughout the summer. While some events take place inside the cave, most occur in its gardens. | **Dates:** July and August | **BRUNCH ELECTRONIC:** Brunch Electronic, one of Malaga's largest electronic music festivals, presents over 40 artists during spring and autumn. Held at the Auditorio Municipal Cortijo de Torres, the events offer over 12 hours of music, food trucks, and bars. | **Dates:** April & May | **SELVATIC FEST MÁLAGA:** This summer festival at the old Drive-In Cinema Malaga boasts around thirty performances spanning various genres like flamenco soul, urban rap, and reggaeton. The event includes a gastronomic area and a market featuring local artisans. **Dates:** June to September | **HÍBRIDA FESTIVAL MÁLAGA:** Híbrida Festival showcases hard techno and breakbeat genres at the former Drive-In Cinema. With two dedicated stages hosting national and international artists, the festival promises a unique musical experience. Date: March 16th

These are just a few highlights of the vibrant music scene in and around Málaga in 2024. Whether you're into electronic beats, classical melodies, or indie tunes, there's something for every music lover to enjoy.

MALAGA ANNUAL EVENTS CALENDAR

JANUARY
1st January - New Year's Day (National holiday).
5-6th January – Three Kings Day: A significant event for Spanish children, featuring parades and gift-giving by the Three Kings.

FEBRUARY
From 23rd February – Annual carnivals celebrated across Spain, with Cadiz hosting the most famous one.
28th February - Day of Andalucia: State holiday commemorating the region with traditional activities.

MARCH OR APRIL
Easter Week: Known as Semana Santa, marked by religious processions throughout Spain, particularly noteworthy in Malaga.

MAY
1st May – Labor Day: Recognized with a national holiday in Spain.
3rd May - Cruces de Mayo: Celebrated with flower-decorated crosses, especially in the Granada area.

JUNE
18th June - Corpus Christi: Religious processions held in Malaga.
23rd June - San Juan: Beach parties and bonfires marking the summer solstice.

JULY
16th July - Virgen del Carmen: Coastal towns celebrate their patron saint of the sea with ceremonies and processions.

AUGUST
Mid-August – Malaga's traditional annual fair, featuring festivities, concerts, and flamenco dresses.
15th August - Asunción de la Virgen: National holiday honoring the patron

of Spain.

19th August - Local holiday in Malaga Province for San Cririaco y Santa Paula.

SEPTEMBER

8th September - Virgen de la Victoria: Local holiday in honor of the city's patron.

OCTOBER

12th October - Dia de la Hispanidad: National holiday commemorating Christopher Columbus's arrival in America.

NOVEMBER

1st November – All Saints' Day: A national holiday to honor and remember the deceased.

DECEMBER

6th December – Constitution Day: National holiday marking the signing of the Spanish Constitution.

8th December - Inmaculada Concepción: National holiday honoring the patron of Spain.

25th December - Christmas Day: Celebrated with presents from Santa, though Three Kings Day is more traditional.

28th December - Los Santos Inocentes: Similar to April Fool's Day, marked by pranks and festivities.

CHAPTER 6: ACCOMMODATION: 25 BEST PLACES

Malaga offers a wide range of lodging options catering to diverse budgets and preferences. From luxurious beachfront resorts like the Gran Hotel Miramar GL to budget-friendly establishments like the Malaga Premium Hotel, there's something for everyone. Holiday rentals, including apartments and villas, provide space and privacy in various locations from the city center to beachside neighborhoods. Hostels are perfect for budget-conscious travelers, fostering social connections and organizing activities. For a rustic experience, Malaga has campsites catering to tent camping, caravans, and motorhomes, offering an alternative amidst nature. When selecting your accommodation in Malaga, Consider: **Location:** Determine whether you prefer staying in the vibrant city center, near the beach, or in a tranquil residential area. **Budget:** Establish your accommodation budget to align with your financial plan. **Amenities:** Identify the amenities that are essential to your stay, such as a swimming pool, spa facilities, or fitness center. **Travel Style:** Consider your travel companions and preferences, whether traveling solo, as a couple, or with family.

BEST LUXURY HOTELS IN MALAGA

1. AC HOTEL MALAGA PALACIO: With stunning views of the Alcazaba & the Castillo de Gibralfaro, the AC Hotel in Malaga offers luxurious accommodations, complete with a remarkable rooftop terrace and exceptional restaurant. Located just minutes away from the Malaga Cathedral, and within easy reach of the port for breathtaking sunsets, convenience is at your fingertips. After a day of hiking, indulge in some leisurely exploration along the Larios shopping street, where you can pamper yourself with fashionable finds or delectable tapas. All these experiences await just steps away from your hotel.

2. GRAN HOTEL MIRAMAR GL: in Malaga offers luxury steps from La Malagueta Beach. Housed in a historic 20th-century building, it boasts elegant rooms with modern amenities like flat-screen TVs and Bulgari toiletries. Enjoy dining at Príncipe de Asturias or drinks on the rooftop terrace with sea views. Features include a spa, pools, and conference rooms. Its prime location offers easy access to attractions and Malaga Airport. Couples love it for romantic getaways. Amenities include private parking, free WiFi, and beachfront access. Part of the Hoteles Santos chain, it's known for excellent breakfast and comfy beds, ideal for luxury and relaxation seekers in Malaga.

3. VINCCI SELECCIÓN ALEYSA: is a luxurious beachfront boutique hotel in Benalmádena, Spain, offering stunning Mediterranean Sea views. Modern rooms feature amenities like air conditioning, LED TVs, & elegant bathrooms. Guests can relax in the outdoor pool & hot tub, with direct access to Las Gaviotas beach. Free sports classes & courtesy cars are available. The on-site restaurant caters to international cuisine and celiacs, complemented by a snack bar and lounge-bar. Nearby attractions include Puerto Marina and Torrequebrada Golf Course. Couples love its romantic setting. Popular amenities include two pools, free WiFi, a spa, and a private beach area.

MID-RANGE ACCOMMODATION IN MALAGA

4. PALACIO SOLECIO: Situated next to a 16th-century church in Málaga's Jewish Quarter, close to attractions like the Alcazaba and Picasso Museum. Housed in an 18th-century Andalusian palace, offering chic rooms with modern amenities. The on-site restaurant, led by Michelin-star chef José Carlos, serves avant-garde cuisine. Guests can enjoy a variety of room categories, some with unique features like Juliette balconies, soaking tubs, Grand staircase entrance, inner courtyard, vintage lighting, and proximity to historic landmarks.

5. ICON MALABAR: Located in the trendy SOHO district of Málaga, close to the marina, waterfront, and city attractions like the Cathedral and Alcazaba. Occupying a historic building from the early 20th century, the hotel offers bright and spacious rooms with a tranquil vibe. The on-site restaurant, Café Salsamente, serves Mediterranean cuisine inspired by the city's Roman past. It offers shuttered Juliette balconies, daily breakfast buffet focusing on healthy foods, and proximity to bars, cafés, and restaurants.

6. ROOM MATE VALERIA HOTEL: Positioned at the edge of the SOHO district, near the marina & Old Town, with easy access to city sites & attractions. Offers basic rooms, standard rooms, and suites with a theme inspired by the area's natural environment. Rooftop terrace with heated pool & sea views, breakfast buffet until noon, and a gym. It offers restored 18th and 19th-century façades, jungle-themed interiors, and proximity to the marina and Paseo del Muelle Uno.

7. MOLINA LARIO HOTEL: Situated at the end of Calle Molina Lario, near Málaga Park and the waterfront promenade Paseo del Muelle Uno, offering a blend of old and new attractions. It combines two historic buildings with a modern Art Deco style, featuring a gourmet restaurant, rooftop terrace with swimming pool, and sea views. Rooms are bright and modern, with options for families. It offers original façades, gourmet dining at Matiz restaurant, and proximity to the Cathedral, Picasso Museum, and other city landmarks.

8. HOTEL PALACETE DE ALAMOS: Located near Plaza de la Merced, Teatro

Romano, and the Alcazaba, offering easy access to city exploration. A historic hotel with unique charms like exposed brick walls and tile flooring, featuring a daily breakfast buffet and a beautiful spa area with a heated pool and sauna. Rooms include unique elements like Jacuzzi tubs and private balconies. It offers quaint dining room with antique furniture, spa services, and proximity to city attractions and restaurants.

9. PARADOR DE MÁLAGA GIBRALFARO: Situated next to Castillo de Gibralfaro, offering panoramic views of the city's waterfront, marina, and Old Town. A historic hilltop stone structure with traditional elements, spacious rooms with private balconies, and a restaurant terrace with stunning views. Outdoor swimming pool, daily breakfast buffet, and on-site parking. It offers Incredible vistas, proximity to the castle, and traditional Spanish architecture.

BEST BUDGET FRIENDLY ACCOMMODATION IN MALAGA

10. HOTEL SOLYMAR: Located in Málaga, Spain, just steps from the beach, Hotel Solymar offers modern accommodations with amenities like air conditioning and free WiFi. Guests appreciate the 24-hour reception and proximity to transportation hubs and the city center. Couples love its romantic setting. Facilities include private parking and disabled access.

11. OHO BOUTIQUE LAS VEGAS: Overlooking La Malagueta Beach in Malaga, Spain, Soho Boutique Las Vegas features spacious rooms with private balconies and amenities like free WiFi. Guests enjoy the poolside breakfast buffet and outdoor pool. Limited parking is available on site. Nearby attractions include Málaga Cathedral and the Picasso Museum.

12. HOTEL LA CHANCLA: Set in Málaga, Spain, Hotel La Chancla offers a charming beachfront stay in the city's traditional fishing neighborhood. Guests can relax on the sun terrace or enjoy the hot tub and terrace bar. Couples love the romantic atmosphere. Facilities include parking, free WiFi, and a restaurant with a wonderful breakfast.

13. ADEINTERRANEA SUITES: Just 2.8 km from Misericordia Beach, Madeinterranea Suites is a cozy budget hotel offering allergy-free rooms and a continental breakfast. Located near the Jorge Rando Museum and Gibralfaro Viewpoint, it provides a comfortable retreat with modern amenities.

FAMILY-FRIENDLY PLACES TO STAY IN MALAGA

15. BARCELO MALAGA is a top-rated family-friendly hotel in Malaga, located at C/ Heroe De Sostoa 2, offering various amenities such as Wi-Fi, luggage storage, 24-hour reception, a poolside snack bar, a restaurant, and more, starting from $109 per night. Situated 1.5 km from La Calle Larios, this unique hotel boasts a sauna, solarium, and sundeck, providing easy access to attractions like the CAC Malaga and Parque de Malaga.

16. VENECIA HOTEL, located at Alameda Principal 9, offers free Wi-Fi, a 24-hour reception, a bar/lounge area, and a restaurant, starting from $53 per night. With its proximity to the ancient Roman Theatre and Parque de Malaga, it provides a convenient stay for guests.

17. NOVOTEL SUITES MALAGA CENTRO, situated at Calle San Jacinto 7, offers amenities like Wi-Fi, a 24-hour reception, a bar/lounge area, & a fitness centre, starting from $121 per night. Its location near Mercado Central de Atarazanas & Museo Carmen Thyssen Malaga makes it an excellent choice for budget-conscious families.

18. ILUNION MALAGA, located at Paseo Maritimo Antonio Machado 10, offers amenities such as Wi-Fi, luggage storage, a 24-hour reception, & an outdoor swimming pool, starting from $122 per night. Its convenient location near Museo Carmen Thyssen Malaga & Parque de Malaga makes it ideal for adults seeking a budget-friendly stay.

19. NH MALAGA HOTEL, situated at Calle San Jacinto 2, offers amenities like Wi-Fi, luggage storage, a locker room, and a rooftop pool, starting from $121 per night. With its unique location and facilities such as a sun terrace and sauna, it provides a comfortable stay for families.

BEST BOUTIQUE HOTELS

20. HOTEL LARIOS MÁLAGA

A boutique hotel with Art Deco design in central Málaga, Spain, close to the Picasso Museum. Offers free WiFi, LCD TVs, and rooms with street views. Guests enjoy a breakfast buffet until noon and a rooftop bar with city views. Popular for romantic getaways.

21. MARIPOSA HOTEL MÁLAGA

Features striking rooms with art deco-style design, located near Calle Larios shopping street. Offers a buffet breakfast until noon, air-conditioned rooms with mini-bars, and chic décor. Close to old town attractions and transport hubs. Popular for romantic getaways.

22. BOUTIQUE CASTILLO DE SANTA CATALINA

Housed in a historic building with unique décor, offering rooms with plasma TVs and stunning views of Málaga Bay. Located in El Limonar, close to La Caleta Beach and city center attractions. Features include free WiFi, outdoor swimming pool, and a restaurant. Popular for romantic getaways.

BEST BEACH RESORTS NEAR MALAGA

23. LA ZAMBRA RESORT GL – MIJAS: nestled in the heart of the stunning Andalusian countryside. As part of The Unbound Collection by Hyatt, this luxurious haven offers exceptional amenities including two outdoor pools, a children's pool, and a top-notch spa. With premium bedding and 24-hour room service, guests can indulge in ultimate comfort. Enjoy delicious buffet breakfasts and dine in style at the on-site restaurants. Plus, with pet-friendly accommodations, everyone can join in the luxury experience.

24. ARBELLA CLUB HOTEL · GOLF RESORT & SPA – MARBELLA: renowned for its Mediterranean charm and stellar amenities. From lush gardens to exquisitely designed rooms, every detail exudes elegance. Families can enjoy a range of activities including a kid's club and pony rides, while spa-goers can unwind with rejuvenating treatments. Strategically located near various attractions, this resort offers the perfect blend of tranquility and adventure.

25. ETT HOTEL & BEACH RESORT MARBELLA – ESTEPONA: offers stunning views & amenities for families. Spacious rooms, engaging kids' club activities, & a relaxing pool area make it an ideal choice for a memorable getaway. Easy access to nearby attractions ensures a fulfilling experience for guests of all ages, while the onsite MOI Spa provides tailored treatments for ultimate relaxation.

26. RAN HOTEL MIRAMAR RESORT & SPA – MALAGA: Indulge in luxury at Gran Hotel Miramar Resort & Spa, where impeccable decor meets exceptional facilities. From fully-equipped spa facilities to breathtaking ocean views, every aspect of this resort promises an unforgettable experience. Located in the heart of Malaga, guests can easily explore top attractions before retreating to the tranquility of this authentic Spanish gem.

CHAPTER 7: TOP 10 OUTDOOR ACTIVITIES TO ENJOY IN MALAGA

1. HIKING IN COSTA DEL SOL: Hiking in the Costa del Sol region of Malaga Province offers stunning coastal views and a variety of trails suitable for different fitness levels. Essential items for hikers include hiking poles and layered clothing due to potential weather changes.

2. ROCK CLIMBING IN EL CHORRO: El Chorro is renowned for both its famous El Caminito del Rey and its rock climbing opportunities. Climbers can enjoy challenging routes along the Desfiladero de Los Gaitanes Gorge, with stunning views along the way.

3. EXPLORING MINAS DE LA TRINIDAD CAVES IN BENALMADENA: Minas de la Trinidad caves provide an exciting adventure just a short walk from the Stupa of Enlightenment in Benalmadena. Visitors should bring a headlamp for exploration and follow painted indicators inside the caves for safety.

4. TRAIL RUNNING IN COSTA DEL SOL: The Sierra de Tejada, Almijara y Alhama Natural Park offers numerous trails for trail runners, including the challenging Pico del Cielo route. Other scenic trail running locations include Sierra Blanca behind Marbella and Sierra de Mijas.

5. CYCLING IN TORREMOLINOS: Cycling enthusiasts can explore mountain tracks behind Torremolinos, with routes leading to viewpoints like Mirador del Lobo. Cyclists should be cautious of processionary caterpillars between late December and May to avoid allergic reactions.

6. BEACH VOLLEYBALL IN FUENGIROLA: Fuengirola's beaches offer a perfect setting for beach volleyball, attracting both locals and tourists during the summer months. It's a fun way to enjoy the beach and make new friends while staying active.

7. KITE SURFING IN ESTEPONA: Guadalmansa beach in Estepona provides excellent conditions for kite surfing year-round, with warm waters in summer and consistent winds. Beginners can take lessons at kite surfing schools in the area.

8. STAND-UP PADDLE BOARDING AND SNORKELING IN NERJA: Nerja's coastline, particularly along Maro, offers pristine waters ideal for stand-up paddle boarding and snorkeling. Exploring hidden beaches and underwater caves is a popular activity during the summer.

9. KAYAKING IN EL CHORRO: The turquoise lakes of El Chorro are perfect for kayaking, offering opportunities for swimming, picnicking, and cliff jumping. Visitors should remember to apply sunscreen due to the strong sun exposure.

10. SCUBA DIVING IN NERJA: Nerja's coast, including the Acantilados de Maro-Cerro Gordo Natural Park, boasts unique diving spots with diverse marine life. Diving centers in Nerja offer PADI courses for beginners interested in exploring the underwater world.

CHAPTER 8: SHOPPING & SOUVENIRS

Shopping and souvenir hunting in Malaga can be quite an enjoyable experience, blending traditional charm with modern convenience. Enhancing your Malaga experience can be achieved by selecting a few souvenirs to commemorate your trip. Below are some insights to souvenir shopping in Malaga to help you make the most of it.

LOCAL MARKETS: Malaga boasts a variety of markets, such as Atarazanas Market, where you can find fresh produce, seafood, meats, and local delicacies. It's not only a great place to shop but also to experience the vibrant local atmosphere. | **SHOPPING DISTRICTS:** Calle Larios is the heart of Malaga's shopping scene, lined with boutiques, fashion stores, and cafes. You'll find both popular international brands and unique local shops offering clothing, accessories, and more. | **ARTISANAL CRAFTS:** Look out for artisanal shops scattered around the city, particularly in the historic center. These offer handmade crafts, ceramics, jewelry, and traditional Spanish goods, perfect for unique souvenirs. | **LOCAL PRODUCTS:** Don't miss the chance to sample and purchase local products such as olive oil, wine, cheese, and cured meats. These items make for excellent gifts or personal mementos of your time in Malaga. | **ANTIQUES AND VINTAGE FINDS:** Malaga is also home to antique shops and vintage stores, where you can unearth treasures ranging from furniture to artwork and collectibles. | **BEACHSIDE SOUVENIRS:** If you're spending time along the coast, you'll find numerous shops selling beachwear, towels, sun hats, and other seaside essentials, along with souvenir shops offering trinkets and memorabilia. | **SHOPPING MALLS**: Malaga has several malls like Centro Comercial Larios Centro and Centro Comercial Vialia. Here, you'll find a wide range of shops, restaurants, and entertainment options under one roof.

SOURVENIR TO BUY

CERAMICS: In Malaga, ceramics are deeply intertwined with local tradition, particularly the renowned malagueno pottery. Crafted with intricate designs & vibrant colors, these ceramics reflect the rich history & culture of the region, making them truly distinctive. Among the noteworthy souvenirs are "azulejos," painted tiles adorning buildings, & "botijos," traditional water pitchers adorned with elaborate patterns, perfect for keeping beverages cool.

JEWELRY: Malaga boasts a rich tradition of silver and goldsmithing, offering a plethora of exquisite jewelry inspired by Andalusian motifs. Filigree, a delicate metalwork style, is a prominent feature in many pieces. For those seeking vibrancy, jewelry adorned with Malaga turquoise stone, renowned for its unique blue-green hue, presents an attractive option. Additionally, traditional Spanish fans, adorned with colorful designs depicting floral patterns or flamenco scenes, offer both functionality and artistic appeal.

TEXTILES: Textiles in Malaga are a testament to local craftsmanship, ranging from T-shirts to handmade bags & decorative folding fans. Crafted by skilled artisans, these items offer something special for every visitor. Flamenco dresses, a quintessential symbol of Spanish culture, come in diverse designs, each handcrafted with care by local artisans. Another popular textile souvenir is the "Manton de Manila," a vibrant shawl made from silk or cotton, featuring intricate embroidered or printed patterns, perfect for adding flair to any outfit

Food-related Souvenir: For food enthusiasts, Malaga offers a delectable array of souvenirs, from traditional sweets like mantecados, almond-based cookies enjoyed during the holidays, to sweet wines made from Moscatel grapes using traditional methods. Malaga's olive oil, renowned for its exceptional quality & numerous awards, is a sought-after souvenir, reflecting the region's culinary excellence.

TOP 15 THINGS TO BUY AS SOUVENIR

OLIVE OIL: Màlaga, with its abundant olive groves, offers a perfect opportunity to procure some top-quality extra-virgin olive oil. Whether you peruse local grocery stores or immerse yourself in the vibrant atmosphere of bustling markets, you'll find a variety of options. Consider enhancing your experience by taking a tour of a nearby olive mill to sample the oil firsthand. Remember to keep your purchases, including olive oil and other delicacies, sealed until you return home.

ANDALUSIAN CERAMICS Andalusian ceramics are a hallmark of Spain's artisanal tradition, particularly renowned for their vibrant pottery. In Màlaga, you'll discover a plethora of ceramic treasures ranging from kitchen essentials like plates and mugs to decorative pieces such as religious crosses and hand-painted tiles. Each item adds a touch of charm to any home décor.

PICASSO SOUVENIRS: Pay homage to Pablo Picasso's legacy by exploring the plethora of Picasso-themed souvenirs scattered throughout Màlaga, the artist's birthplace. A visit to the Picasso Museum followed by a browse through the onsite gift shop offers a delightful way to commemorate your journey with items like books, posters, or colorful tote bags.

WINE: Màlaga boasts an array of affordable yet delightful wines, perfect for wine enthusiasts seeking a memorable taste of Spain. Whether you fancy a local sweet dessert wine or Spain's equivalent of champagne, known as cava, you're sure to find a bottle to suit your palate. Just remember the duty-free alcohol allowance for cruise passengers.

MUSCATEL RAISINS: Treat your taste buds to the exquisite flavor of muscatel raisins from southern Spain. These plump, sun-dried delicacies offer a sweetness that surpasses store-bought alternatives, making them an ideal souvenir to share with loved ones back home.

TAPAS BOWLS: Dive into the world of Spanish cuisine by indulging in tapas, small plates of delectable dishes served in bars and cafes across Spain. To recreate this culinary experience at home, consider investing in traditional terracotta tapas bowls, ensuring an authentic touch to your homemade tapas feast.

PAELLA PAN: Elevate your culinary repertoire with the iconic Spanish dish, paella, by acquiring a high-quality paella pan from Màlaga. Crafted to perfection, this traditional pan is essential for mastering the art of preparing this beloved comfort food.

SAFFRON: Don't forget to stock up on saffron, the prized spice essential for infusing Spanish dishes with rich flavor. While it may be more expensive elsewhere, purchasing saffron in Spain ensures both quality and authenticity, enhancing your culinary creations.

SPANISH BULL PRODUCTS: Immerse yourself in the cultural heritage of Andalusia with Spanish bull products, reminiscent of the region's historic connection to bullfighting. From souvenir shops brimming with bullfighting memorabilia to charming keepsakes like stuffed bull toys and themed apparel, there's no shortage of mementos to commemorate your visit.

FLAMENCO MUSIC: Experience the soul-stirring rhythms of flamenco music with a captivating CD featuring this expressive art form. Whether you're reliving the magic of a live performance or discovering flamenco for the first time, this musical souvenir promises to evoke memories of your Spanish adventure.

FLAMENCO DRESS: Embrace the elegance of Andalusian tradition with a flamenco dress, a symbol of cultural pride and artistic expression. Browse specialized shops in Màlaga to find the perfect flamenco attire, characterized by its flamboyant design and cascading ruffles.

FLAMENCO CASTANETS: Capture the essence of flamenco with a pair of castanets, the iconic percussion instrument synonymous with Spanish dance. These intricately crafted wooden pieces add a rhythmic flair to any performance and serve as a cherished reminder of your cultural immersion.

MANTILLA (SPANISH VEIL): Enhance your wardrobe with the timeless elegance of a mantilla, a delicate Spanish veil worn for various social occasions. Available in a variety of styles, these lace veils exude sophistication and grace, reflecting centuries of tradition and refinement.

SPANISH FAN: Stay cool in the Màlaga heat with a vibrant Spanish fan, adorned with intricate designs inspired by nature and folklore. Whether used for practical purposes or displayed as decorative art, these handcrafted fans capture the essence of Spanish culture and craftsmanship.

BIZNAGA: Take a piece of Màlaga's summertime charm home with porcelain replicas of biznagas, fragrant floral arrangements crafted from dried thistle and jasmine. While you can't bring the fresh blooms aboard your cruise, these exquisite souvenirs offer a lasting reminder of your Spanish sojourn.

TOP 8 SHOPPING AREA

1. CALLE LARIOS: For a quintessential European shopping experience featuring beloved brands like Mango & Zara, Calle Larios is your go-to spot. This central shopping street, officially known as Calle Marqués de Larios, boasts an elegant marble pathway & seasonal decorations, such as enchanting Christmas lights. Peruse the array of clothing, lingerie, cosmetics, & banking services available, then treat yourself to a coffee or ice cream at Lepanto cafeteria as you soak in the lively atmosphere. With operating hours from 10am to 9pm, Calle Larios promises a vibrant shopping adventure throughout the day. | **2. CALLE NUEVA**" Parallel to Calle Larios, Calle Nueva offers a bustling alternative with a mix of Spanish and international brands. Whether you're hunting for high-end fashion or quirky gifts, this pedestrianized street delivers. To beat the crowds, consider visiting in the early morning or during the Spanish lunchtime break from 2 to 4 pm. Calle Nueva's charming ambiance and diverse selection of shops make it a must-visit for a truly local shopping experience. | **3. CALLE ESPECERÍA/CISNEROS:** Immerse yourself in authentic Spanish fashion along Calle Especería, transitioning into Calle Cisneros. Lined with historic buildings, this narrow thoroughfare showcases chic clothing, flamenco attire, and traditional footwear from both large retailers and family-owned boutiques. Indulge in a culinary delight at Golden Tips or Empanadas Malvón, or recharge with a Starbucks break at Plaza de la Constitución. Remember that many smaller shops close for lunch between 2 and 5 pm, so plan accordingly to make the most of your shopping excursion. | **4. CALLE COMPAÑÍA:** Discover a blend of independent stores, cozy bars, and inviting cafes along Calle Compañía, nestled parallel to Calle Especería and near Calle Larios. From unique gifts at the Carmen Thyssen Museum shop to vintage finds at JOAN Vintage Charity Shop, this picturesque street caters to various interests. After browsing, indulge in international cuisine at nearby restaurants, offering Greek, Italian, Thai, Spanish, or vegan options. Calle Compañía invites you to immerse yourself in its historical charm, eclectic shops, and delightful dining spots. | **5. CALLE ANDRÉS PÉREZ:** Uncover hidden treasures along the narrow lanes of Calle Andrés Pérez, located off Plaza de los Mártires. With its recent revamp, this street boasts unique boutiques, art galleries, tea shops, and antique stores. Explore *La Casa del Cardenal* for antique wonders or indulge in traditional tapas at *Las Merchanas 2*. For a dose of artistry, visit the *Mahatma Showroom*, filled with children's toys and artwork. Don't miss the enchanting *Vertical en la Plaza del Pericón Garden* tucked away on Calle Pozos Dulces. | **6. ALAGA ATARAZANAS MARKET (MERCADO DE ATARAZANAS):** Malaga's markets are prime spots for souvenir hunting, showcasing local products like fresh produce & handcrafted goods. The renowned Malaga Atarazanas Market, housed in a striking 19th-century structure, immerses visitors in bustling atmospheres & authentic experiences. Textiles and leather goods are particularly abundant, making browsing through the stalls a memorable experience. | **7. SOHO DISTRICT: ALTERNATIVE SOUVENIR SHOPPING:** For a more unique shopping experience, the Soho district offers independent shops and boutiques featuring handmade jewelry, clothing, and artisanal products. This trendy neighborhood also hosts galleries and art spaces where visitors can discover one-of-a-kind ceramics, glassware, and decorative items. | **8. BEACH PROMENADE:** Another popular destination for souvenir shopping, with shops offering beach towels, sun hats, and other essentials for a day by the sea. You can also find souvenirs showcasing Malaga's beautiful beaches and coastline, perfect for capturing memories of your time in the city.

TOP 10 SHOPPING CENTRES & MALLS

1. CENTRO COMERCIAL LARIOS CENTRO: Immerse yourself in the bustling atmosphere of Centro Comercial Larios Centro, just a short 15-minute walk from Málaga's heart. Recently renovated, this two-story mall boasts a plethora of popular global brands like Zara, H&M, and Primark. Satisfy your cravings at various dining spots, including 100 Montaditos and McDonald's. Convenient parking and air conditioning enhance your comfort during your visit.

2. MUELLE UNO: Experience the vibrant ambiance of Muelle Uno, nestled in the picturesque Port of Málaga. Browse high-end stores like Lacoste and enjoy culinary delights amidst stunning harbor views. Live music, exhibitions, and scenic walks along the waterfront add to the allure of this open-air destination.

3. VIALIA CENTRO COMERCIAL: Conveniently linked to Málaga María Zambrano Train Station, Vialia Centro Comercial offers modernity and convenience. Explore 80+ stores, including Calzedonia and Media Markt, before indulging in a meal at Taco Bell or McDonald's. Entertainment options abound, from a 13-screen cinema to an indoor playground for the little ones.

4. PLAZA MAYOR: Embark on a shopping adventure at Plaza Mayor, a spacious open-air mall near Málaga-Costa del Sol Airport. Renowned brands like Nike and Oysho await, alongside a diverse dining scene. Don't miss the adjacent McArthur Glen Outlet Mall for unbeatable discounts on luxury brands.

5. MCARTHURGLEN DESIGNER OUTLET MÁLAGA: Adjacent to Plaza Mayor, discover the ultimate destination for designer bargains. Shop over 100 brands, including Prada and Calvin Klein, at discounts up to 70% off. Recharge at nearby restaurants like Five Guys before continuing your shopping spree.

6. EL CORTE INGLÉS MÁLAGA: Immerse yourself in the iconic Spanish department store experience at El Corte Inglés. Browse an extensive range of products, from fashion to household essentials, and savor culinary delights at the Gourmet Experience. Don't miss the biannual sales for incredible savings.

7. CENTRO COMERCIAL ROSALEDA: Located near the Rosaleda soccer stadium, this mall offers a mix of Spanish and European fashion retailers, along with essential services like a hair salon and a Carrefour supermarket. Limited dining options include McDonald's and Pomodoro, ensuring a convenient shopping experience.

8. CENTRO COMERCIAL LOS PATIOS: Experience a relaxed shopping environment at Centro Comercial Los Patios, featuring around 40 stores, eateries, and recreational spaces. Enjoy Andalusian-inspired architecture and easy accessibility via public transportation.

9. MÁLAGA FACTORY/PARQUE COMERCIAL MÁLAGA NOSTRUM: Score deals at Málaga Factory, offering discounted Spanish retailers and renowned brands like Mango and Desigual. Dine at eateries like Burger King before catching a movie at the onsite theater.

10. MÁLAGA PLAZA: Nestled next to El Corte Inglés, Centro Comercial Málaga Plaza offers a modest selection of stores and services, including a 24-hour parking facility. Delight in the architectural charm and occasional events at this central Málaga destination.

TOP TIPS FOR SOUVENIR SHOPPING

1. PRIORITIZE AUTHENTICITY: Focus on handcrafted items that truly reflect Malaga's culture and history, steering clear of mass-produced trinkets. Explore local markets like Atarazanas or the artistic Soho district for one-of-a-kind finds. | **2. DELIGHT IN LOCAL FLAVORS:** Treat yourself to the flavors of Malaga with delectable edible souvenirs. From savory treats like olives and salchichón to sweet delights like turrón, indulge your palate at places like Atarazanas Market or specialty shops such as La Mallorquina or Ultramarinos Zoilo. | **3. EMBRACE FLAMENCO VIBES:** Immerse yourself in Malaga's flamenco culture by bringing home flamenco-inspired items like castanets, fans, or even traditional clothing. Consider browsing the Cudeca charity shops for budget-friendly flamenco dresses. | **4. SUPPORT COMMUNITY BUSINESSES:** Look out for the "Málaga de Calidad" label to ensure your purchases support local artisans and businesses, guaranteeing authenticity and quality. | **5. BARGAIN SMARTLY:** Embrace the art of negotiation at flea markets and street vendors, a common practice in Spain. Approach haggling respectfully and you might snag some surprising deals. | **6. CONSIDER PRACTICALITY:** Keep practicality in mind when selecting souvenirs, especially if you're tight on luggage space. Opt for lightweight items or those easily packable to avoid any travel hassles. | **7. MIND OPENING HOURS:** Be aware of siesta breaks, during which many shops close between 2 pm and 5 pm. Plan your shopping excursions accordingly to make the most of your time and avoid disappointment. **8. ENJOY THE JOURNEY:** Souvenir shopping isn't just about the items you acquire but also the experience itself. Take pleasure in exploring different shops, interacting with locals, and immersing yourself in Malaga's vibrant culture.

CHAPTER 9: NIGHTLIFE & ENTERTAINMENT

Thanks to its abundance of Spanish language schools and one of Andalusia's largest university campuses, Málaga attracts a youthful, vibrant crowd. While Barcelona holds the title of "party city" with a more upscale and tourist-centric nightlife, Málaga offers a student-friendly, laid-back yet equally exhilarating experience. Whether you fancy relaxing in traditional tapas bars, dancing the night away in modern clubs, or sipping fancy cocktails, Málaga caters to every taste. This chapter will lead you through the top party neighborhoods, clubs, bars, and cocktail hot spots in Málaga.

WHAT TO EXPECT FROM MÁLAGA'S NIGHTLIFE

Málaga's nightlife scene is everything a young reveler could desire. The streets of this Cultural Capital of the Costa del Sol pulse with locals and young expats hopping from one bar to another, savoring local Málaga dulce and enjoying vibrant music. Expect to be surrounded by a friendly, relaxed crowd. Typically, the night kicks off with pre-drinks at home, followed by exploration of the city's wine cellars, taverns, and trendy tapas bars. After midnight, it's time to hit the nightclubs. As a general rule, Málaga's nightlife starts late and wraps up in the early hours of the morning. Fortunately, getting home after a night of revelry is hassle-free, with most bars in the city center within walking distance. Additionally, Málaga boasts an extensive and affordable public transportation system to swiftly and safely transport partygoers to other nightlife hotspots.

TOP NEIGHBORHOODS FOR PARTYING IN MÁLAGA

CENTER OF MÁLAGA/CENTRO HISTÓRICO: The heart of Málaga hosts most of its nightlife, particularly around Plaza de la Merced and Plaza de Uncibay. Charming streets are lined with clubs and bars that stay open until the early hours of the morning. With reasonably priced bars, this area is popular among locals and students. Pro tip: Arrive early for discounted drinks.

LA MERCED: The birthplace of Picasso, La Merced is a lively district within walking distance of Centro Histórico. After pre-drinks in the square, explore its famous streets, Calle Carreteria and Calle Alamo, which are dotted with renowned clubs and discos open late into the night.

LA MALAGUETA: Located near the port and city center, La Malagueta is a bustling beach neighborhood popular among younger crowds, especially during the summer. It boasts numerous tapas restaurants, bars, rooftops, and beach bars, along with some of Málaga's premier clubs.

EL PALO Y PEDREGALEJO: Pedregalejo boasts Málaga's liveliest student nightlife, offering everything from traditional tapas bars to hip clubs. Its proximity to the University of Málaga campus makes it a top choice for students, and it's easily accessible from the city center via public transportation.

THE PORT OF MÁLAGA: For a laid-back evening, head to the Port of Málaga, surrounding one of Spain's oldest ports. While options may be limited, you'll find charming cocktail bars offering beautiful views. Accessible by shuttle bus or solar train from the center, this area provides a relaxed atmosphere for unwinding.

THE BEST NIGHT CLUBS IN MÁLAGA

PACHA COSTA DEL SOL stands out as one of Malaga's largest and most popular nightclubs, boasting a capacity of 1800 enthusiastic partygoers. The club primarily features deep house music, with lounge music also available for those seeking a more relaxed atmosphere. Designed by the renowned Spanish designer Jorge Goula, the club's notable features include its boat-shaped bar, offering an array of fancy cocktails and beverages. | **Operating hours:** Thursday through Saturday, from midnight until 7 a.m. | **Location:** Parque de Oclo Plaza Mayor, s/n. | 29004, Málaga

BUBBLES MALAGA offers a more laid-back ambiance compared to Pacha Costa del Sol. Situated in the heart of Malaga, it serves as a chic lounge bar often featuring live music performances. Alongside live music, the venue plays various genres, including salsa, R&B, Spanish, and international music. Female dancers are occasionally hired to enhance the evening's entertainment, and on Wednesday nights, guests can dance to traditional Spanish salsa. | **Operating hours:** Monday through Sunday, from 4 p.m. to 4 a.m. | **Location:** Calle Mártires 14 | 29008, Málaga

VELVET emerges as one of Malaga's renowned nightclubs, centrally located between the Picasso Museum and the Thyssen Museum. Noteworthy for its dual role as a nightclub and concert hall, Velvet's standout feature is its wooden design, providing a unique aesthetic. Live music performances are a common occurrence, and the venue offers options for room reservations and private parties, ensuring a lively atmosphere every weekend. | **Operating hours:** Monday through Sunday, from 11 p.m. to 6 a.m. | **Location:** Calle de las Comedias 15 | 29008 Málaga

SIEMPRE ASI, situated in Malaga's city center, offers a vibrant Latino club experience. Known for its trendy ambiance and diverse crowd, the club attracts patrons of all ages eager to dance the night away. Notably, Siempre Asi is renowned for its cocktails, often hailed as the best in the city for their generous alcohol content and refreshing flavors. | **Location:** Calle de los Convalencientes 5 | 29008 Málaga

ANDÉN NIGHTCLUB: Andén Nightclub is renowned for its top-notch lighting and sound systems, making it one of Malaga's premier nightlife destinations. Boasting two rooms, four bars, six VIP areas, and 13 screens, this venue ensures an unforgettable experience for revelers. They host a student night every Thursday throughout the academic year, offering a vibrant atmosphere for those keen on a lively night out. Opting for a VIP table grants access to a dedicated team of waitstaff, adding a touch of magic to your evening. Expect a musical lineup predominantly featuring industrial and reggaeton tracks. | **Operating hours**: Every day | **Main music genres:** Latin and Commercial | **Expected entrance fee:** Free - 10€

SALA GOLD: Sala Gold is a renowned nightclub catering to diverse musical tastes. From salsa and bachata to electronic and Spanish pop, the venue offers something for everyone. With different themed nights each day of the week, Sala Gold ensures an enticing lineup to keep patrons coming back for more. Notably, they also feature a Live Sport room for sports enthusiasts to enjoy games while savoring a beer in a relaxed setting. | **Operating hours:** Every day | **Main music genres:** Latin and Commercial | **Expected entrance fee**: 5€ - 9€

SALA WENGÉ: Wengé Privé stands out as another popular nightclub in Malaga, boasting a modern and trendy ambiance accentuated by mirrored walls that enhance the immersion in the music. Hosting parties from Thursday to Saturday, it attracts a youthful crowd aged 20 to 35 eager to dance to the latest R&B and EDM tunes. Offering excellent value for money, Wengé is a must-visit for budget-conscious travelers seeking an unforgettable nightlife experience. | **Operating hours:** Every day

THEATRO CLUB MÁLAGA: Theatro Club Málaga distinguishes itself by focusing on live performances every night of the week, featuring a diverse lineup ranging from burlesque and cabaret to theater plays, jazz sessions, and stand-up comedy. With a decor reminiscent of a small theater, this venue offers a unique clubbing experience where patrons gather around the main stage to enjoy the entertainment. The crowd varies depending on the event, ensuring a dynamic atmosphere for party-goers. | **Operating hours:** Every day | **Main music genres**: Latin and R&B | **Expected entrance fee:** 5€ - 10€

THE FINEST NIGHT BARS IN MÁLAGA

LOLA LOUNGE is a bar that captures the essence of contemporary Malaga. Offering sweeping views of the city, a diverse menu featuring global flavors, and interior aesthetics reminiscent of a high-end design publication, "Lola Lounge" has emerged as the preferred destination for Malaga's youthful and trendy clientele.

NEON BAR introduces a futuristic element to Malaga's nightlife scene. Adorned with vibrant neon lights, captivating digital art displays, and a beverage selection that delves into the realm of molecular mixology, it presents a distinctive and visually captivating experience, perfect for those seeking both novelty and Instagram-worthy moments.

ATLANTIC: A popular spot among students, ATLANTIC hosts weekly parties for Erasmus students, featuring Spanish and international pop music in a lively atmosphere.

LA TRANCA: Renowned for its tapas and traditional Spanish vibe, La Tranca offers a laid-back setting to enjoy small beers or vermouth while soaking in the ambiance.

SPEAKEASY THE PHARMACY: Recognized as one of Spain's best cocktail bars, Speakeasy The Pharmacy impresses with its award-winning bartender, premium cocktails, and soothing jazz music.

ANTIGUA CASA GUARDIA: Picasso's favorite haunt, this historic bodega serves wine from wood barrels in a rustic atmosphere dating back to 1840, offering a nostalgic trip through Málaga's past.

ZZ BAR: Known for its vibrant live music scene, ZZ bar attracts a young crowd with its friendly service, relaxed ambiance, and affordable drinks.

BEST ROOFTOP BARS IN MÁLAGA

TERRAZA DE SAN JUAN: "Terraza de San Juan" epitomizes this elevated experience perfectly. Situated in the city center, this rooftop bar provides awe-inspiring vistas of Malaga's cathedral, the Alcazaba, and the glistening sea beyond. Featuring stylish decor, ambient lighting, and a menu showcasing both local and international flavors, it stands as a preferred destination for those seeking refuge from the city's hustle and bustle while reveling in its splendor.

SKYLINE ROOFTOP BAR: Another notable establishment embracing is "Skyline Rooftop Bar." True to its name, this venue offers unmatched panoramas of Malaga's skyline. Yet, its allure extends beyond the views. Renowned for its inventive cocktails, the bar combines traditional Spanish ingredients with international mixology techniques, crafting beverages that tantalize the taste buds as much as the vistas mesmerize the eyes.

LA TERRAZA OASIS: Situated atop Oasis Backpackers' Hostel, La Terraza Oasis offers a laid-back rooftop experience with live DJ performances and refreshing gin & tonics.

ÀTICO BAR & RESTAURANT: Located on the 15th floor of Málaga Palacio hotel, Àtico Bar & Restaurant offers panoramic views of Gibralfaro castle and the Mediterranean sea, making it an ideal spot for indulging in fancy cocktails and enjoying a romantic atmosphere.

THEATERS, CINEMAS, & OTHER ENTERTAINMENT OPTIONS

If you are inclined towards contemporary entertainment, the city boasts numerous cinemas and theaters to explore.

TEATRO CÁNOVAS: Among the prominent theaters is Teatro Cánovas, a long-standing institution established in 1849 at the heart of Malaga. Here, visitors can enjoy a variety of performances spanning plays, musicals, and dance shows.

SOHO THEATRE: In the Soho Arts District, the revamped Soho Theatre stands as another enticing option. Originally built in 1937, the theater reopened its doors in 2019, showcasing a blend of local and international productions, including plays, stand-up comedy, and musical performances.

CINE ALBÉNIZ: For a classic movie night, Malaga offers several cinemas. Cine Albéniz, situated on Alcazabilla Street, boasts four screens featuring Spanish and international films.

MK2 CINESUR MALAGA NOSTRUM: mk2 Cinesur Málaga Nostrum, located on Azucarera Intelhorce road, is a modern multiplex cinema equipped with 12 screens screening the latest blockbuster hits.

Whether you seek an evening of laughter, thought-provoking drama, or cinematic spectacle, Malaga presents a diverse array of theaters and cinemas tailored to every preference.

CHAPTER 10: 11 UNFORGETTABLE DAY EXCURSIONS FROM MALAGA

Nestled between the Mediterranean Sea to the south and the Sierra de Tejeda mountains to the north, Malaga boasts a breathtaking locale. Enveloped by natural parks, reserves, charming villages, and historic gems like Sevilla, Granada, and Cordoba. Given its coastal position, Malaga experiences considerably milder summer temperatures compared to other Andalusian cities. The disparity is notable, with Cordoba or Seville often hitting 42/43 °C (107/109 °F) in summer, while Malaga averages a more comfortable 28ºC (82ºF) during July and August. <u>Winters are mild</u>, offering warm, sunny days. <u>December and January </u>typically see an average temperature of 17ºC (63ºF), making beach activities still viable. Additionally, shielded by coastal mountains, Malaga encounters far less wind than its regional counterparts. Yet, the key allure of Malaga as a launchpad for day trips is its proximity to an array of captivating destinations. After exploring Southern Spain on numerous occasions, Below are a compiled collection of my top day excursions from Malaga. Explore below unforgettable day trips from Malaga based on your interests:

FOR HISTORY ENTHUSIASTS

RONDA: Discover this captivating town situated on a breathtaking gorge, with an iconic bridge separating the old and new sections. Explore the Alcazaba (Moorish fortress), the Puente Nuevo (new bridge), and the Plaza de Toros (bullring). | **CÓRDOBA:** Immerse yourself in the UNESCO World Heritage Site with the magnificent Mezquita (mosque-cathedral), stroll through the Jewish Quarter's narrow streets, visit the Alcázar (fortress), and savor traditional tapas. **GRANADA:** Marvel at the Alhambra, an exquisite Moorish palace and fortress. Don't miss the Generalife gardens, the Sacromonte caves, and the Albaicín neighborhood.

FOR NATURE LOVERS

EL CAMINITO DEL REY: Embark on a thrilling hike along the "King's Pathway," a narrow cliff-side trail with breathtaking views. | **EL TORCAL DE ANTEQUERA:** Traverse the otherworldly limestone karst landscape, exploring surreal rock formations and enjoying panoramic views. | **NERJA CAVES:** Delve into vast caves housing prehistoric paintings, stunning stalactites, and stalagmites. Take a guided tour through this underground wonderland.

FOR BEACH AFICIONADOS

MARBELLA: Indulge in the glamour of this resort town, featuring beautiful beaches, luxury yachts, and designer shops. Enjoy a stroll along the Paseo Marítimo, relax on the beach, and shop in Puerto Banús. | **NERJA:** Experience a charming mix of sandy beaches, rocky coves, and whitewashed houses. Take a boat trip to the Maro cliffs, visit the Balcón de Europa viewpoint, and savor fresh seafood. | **FUENGIROLA:** Dive into the lively atmosphere of this town with a long sandy beach, a vibrant marina, and a bustling nightlife. Enjoy water sports, beach relaxation, & dinner at beachfront restaurants.

FOR SOMETHING UNIQUE

GIBRALTAR: Explore the British overseas territory blending British and Spanish cultures. Witness the Rock of Gibraltar, encounter Barbary macaques, and take a cable car for panoramic views. | **MIJAS:** Visit this picturesque whitewashed village perched on a hill. Ride a donkey taxi, explore the Plaza de Toros (bullring), and enjoy panoramic views. | **ANTEQUERA:** Discover the historic town renowned for its dolmens (prehistoric tombs). Visit the Alcazaba (fortress), the Colegiata de Santa María la Mayor (collegiate church), and the Roman baths.

MARBELLA

Marbella is a city and municipality in southern Spain, located in the province of Málaga within the autonomous community of Andalusia. It sits on the Costa del Sol, between Málaga and the Strait of Gibraltar, nestled in the foothills of the Sierra Blanca. With an area of 117 square kilometers, it's a hub of tourism, boasting a population of 141,463 in 2018. Marbella's appeal lies in its Mediterranean location, pleasant climate, and robust tourist infrastructure. Beyond tourism, it holds a rich archaeological heritage, numerous museums and performance venues, and a diverse cultural calendar, featuring events ranging from reggae concerts to opera performances. Marbella is renowned for its opulent lifestyle, glamorous marinas, and picturesque beaches, making it a sought-after destination for celebrities, jet-setters, and those in pursuit of a luxurious experience.

HOW TO GET TO MARBELLA

By Car: Hiring a car is the most straightforward option to get to Marbella from Malaga. Driving takes just over an hour via the MA-22 road or a scenic coastal road. Prices for a rental car on Discover Cars range between €35-50 per day. Use N-340/A-7 highway, follow signs for Marbella, and consider navigation apps like Waze or Google Maps. | **By Bus:** Buses run every 30 minutes from Málaga Airport to Marbella. The journey takes 40-45 minutes, costing €6.15 for a normal bus and €8.50 for an express bus. Bus tickets can be prebooked or purchased on the bus. | **By Taxi:** Taxis are available from Malaga to Marbella. Taxis are metered, costing approximately €60-80, payable in Euros or credit/debit cards. Ride-hailing apps like Uber, Cabify, or Free Now can also be considered for potentially better prices. | **Private Transfers:** Suitable for groups or those with more luggage. Private shuttle options for up to 8 people cost €172, while transfers for up to 5 people are €90. | **By Train:** No direct train to Marbella, but you can take the train to Torremolinos and then a bus to Marbella.

MUST-VISIT ATTRACTIONS IN MARBELLA

Fontanilla Beach: Marbella's main beach, Playa de la Fontanilla, features amenities like sun loungers, showers, watersports, and a lively promenade with various dining options. | **Old Town:** Marbella's charming old town, casco antiguo, is a hidden gem with flower-filled streets, romantic squares, and elegant townhouses, reminiscent of Andalusia's oldest cities. | **Plaza de los Naranjos:** The central square in the old town, Plaza de los Naranjos, surrounded by orange trees, offers tapas bars and restaurants with sunny terraces for a relaxing experience. | **Boutiques:** Marbella's old town boasts chic boutiques, adding a touch of modern shopping to its centuries-old architecture.

Divina Pastora: A lively residential neighborhood in central Marbella, Divina Pastora, offers a market, fruit stalls, and a local church with paintings depicting Andalusian provinces. | **Plaza Santo Cristo:** Another attractive square in the old town, Plaza Santo Cristo, features vibrant buildings, including the Ana Maria flamenco bar and the Santo Cristo hermitage. | **Miraflores:** North of casco antiguo, Miraflores is a friendly residential neighborhood with its cultural center housing olive oil and archaeological museums. | **Salvador Dalí Sculptures:** Marbella showcases a world-class collection of Salvador Dalí sculptures along the Avenida del Mar, providing free public art. | **Contemporary Engravings Museum:** The Museo del Grabado Español Contemporaneo, Spain's only museum of its kind, explores the history of Spanish engraving, featuring works by Dalí and Miró.

Puerto Banús: A glamorous marina west of Marbella, Puerto Banús is renowned for luxury yachts, Ferraris, and boutiques, making it a famous Costa del Sol destination. | **Nightlife**: Marbella is globally acclaimed for its vibrant nightlife, with sleek bars in the modern town center, celebrity-packed spots along the Golden Mile, and glitzy nightclubs in Puerto Banús. |

Alameda Park: Parque de Alameda, behind Paseo Maritimo, offers a romantic atmosphere, tiled benches, and a 17th-century fountain, hosting an eco foods market monthly.

Nagüeles Park: Located north of Marbella, Nagüeles National Park provides a spacious recreational area with barbecues, picnic tables, and facilities for dog play and training. | **Constitution Park:** Parque de la Constitución, central Marbella's largest green space, features shady pathways, an auditorium for concerts, and a café for refreshments. | **Castle Walls:** Lower western side of Represa Park houses remnants of Marbella's 9th-century fort, with battered walls and watchtowers from the Moorish period. | **Marbella Market:** Mercado de Marbella, the central food market, offers a glimpse into local street life, with diverse offerings including cheese, wine, fresh meat, and more. | **Culinary Scene:** Marbella boasts four Michelin-starred restaurants, establishing itself as a top culinary destination in Spain, offering a variety of cuisine, especially renowned seafood. | **Divina Pastora Market:** The barrio of Divina Pastora features a colorful and chaotic food market, providing a local experience with fresh fish caught that morning and other diverse goods.

RONDA

Ronda is one of the most picturesque and frequently visited villages in Andalusia. Situated in proximity to Seville (1 hour and 45 minutes by car) and Malaga (1 hour and 30 minutes), it is home to approximately 35,000 residents and is characterized by its cliffside location, a deep canyon carved by the Guadalevín River, and its inclusion in the Sierra de las Nieves National Park. The area holds historical significance with prehistoric settlements and a rich Islamic heritage, evident in its architecture and notable figures like Abbas ibn Firnas. Ronda experienced various conquests, including by the Suebi, Visigoths, and Umayyads, flourishing under Islamic rule until the Reconquista. The El Tajo gorge stands out as Ronda's key feature, dividing the old town from the new, with the iconic Punte Nuevo providing stunning panoramic views. The Arab Baths, dating back to the 12th and 13th centuries, near the Arab Bridge offer a glimpse into Ronda's history. The Plaza de Toros, Spain's oldest bullring, and attractions like Alameda del Tajo and Jardines De Cuenca, along with the Iglesia Santa María la Mayor, contribute to Ronda's rich cultural and historical tapestry. Ronda is easily explored on foot, and a single day is ample to uncover all the must-see attractions and points of interest.

HOW TO GET TO RONDA FROM MALAGA

Driving distance from Malaga: 101.2 km via A-357 and A-367 (1 hr 16 min). To reach Ronda from Malaga, you have several transportation options which include: **Train:** Renfe operates regular trains that offer a scenic journey lasting approximately 1.5 hours. This comfortable mode of transportation provides stunning views of the countryside, making it an enjoyable way to travel. | **Bus:** If you're looking for a budget-friendly option, buses are available and operated by Damas. The journey typically takes around 2 hours and offers convenient access to Ronda. | **Car:** Renting a car provides flexibility & allows you to explore surrounding areas at your leisure. The drive to Ronda takes about 1.5 hours via picturesque routes, offering the opportunity to soak in the scenic beauty along the way. Be aware that the road to Ronda is quite winding & follows the edges of the mountains with numerous zig-zags. If you're not comfortable with this type of driving, it's advisable to entrust the driving to someone else. | **Tours:** Tour is one of the best way to visit Ronda from Malaga. These tours typically include transportation from Malaga & a knowledgeable guide who can provide insights into the town's history.

TOP THINGS TO SEE AND DO IN RONDA

Plaza de Toros de Ronda (Ronda Arena): One of Spain's oldest bullfighting arenas, built in 1785, with a museum showcasing Ronda's bullfighting history. | **Ronda Viewpoint:** Begin from Plaza de Toros and walk along Paseo Blas Infante for breathtaking views of the valley from the cliff's edge. | **Puento Nuevo (New Bridge):** Completed in 1793, this iconic stone bridge connects the old and new town, offering spectacular views. Explore viewpoints at Aldehuela for ideal photo spots. | **Ronda's Mondragón Palace:** Built in 1314, this palace, now Ronda Municipal Museum, displays the village's history and Roman and Arab tombs. The palace gardens provide scenic views.

| **Duchess of Parcent Square:** Visit this beautiful square surrounded by monuments, including the St Mary Major Church, showcasing a blend of Renaissance and Gothic styles. | **The Bandit Museum:** Located near Plaza Duquesa, this museum narrates the history of the region's famous outlaws, including bullfighters, singers, and smugglers. | **Puerta de Almocabar and the Arab Walls:** Explore the former city gate, Puerta de Almocabar, showcasing Ronda's Islamic defensive structures. | **Ronda's Arab Baths:** Located in San Miguel district, these well-preserved 13th-century baths offer insights into Ronda's history. | **La Casa del Rey Moro:** A 14th-century palace with an ingenious water pumping system, featuring a staircase of 236 steps leading to a platform with panoramic views. | **Plaza del Socorro:** Conclude your tour in this charming square, surrounded by bars and restaurants, offering a view of Nuestra Senora del Socorro Church.

BONUS: **The Andalusian Winery in Ronda** has recently been included in the official Andalusian Wine Route. Nestled in nature, numerous small wineries in the region produce exceptional wines that are gaining recognition nationally and internationally. Approximately twenty establishments are part of the wine route, and some offer guided tours of their facilities, complete with wine tastings. The most renowned and frequently visited ones are Chinchilla Bodegas and Descalzos Viejos Bodegas, situated within a convent.

Acinipo, an archaeological site located 20 kilometers from Ronda, served as the former capital of the region before being abandoned in favor of Ronda. The Roman theatre at Acinipo is remarkably well-preserved, with bleachers carved directly into the rock. You can explore various Roman architectural features, as well as remnants of thermal baths and ancient waterworks, all set against a picturesque backdrop of surrounding mountains and the Sierra de Grazalema.

You can visit all the above mentioned places in the recommended order. Ronda is an ideal destination for a day trip from Malaga or Seville, offering the opportunity to explore attractions on foot. The Puente Nuevo, in particular, is awe-inspiring, making Ronda a must-visit location in Andalusia. However, be prepared for the high tourist influx, especially on weekends, leading to elevated prices at restaurants and cafes in the main squares and historic center. **TIP:** If you are a budget-conscious travelers, venture away from the center to find smaller eateries. For instance, *the Granier bakery*, just 100 meters from the Plaza del Socorro, offers sandwiches ranging from 1.50€ to 2.50€, providing a more affordable option compared to the basic sandwich prices starting at 7€ on the nearby main streets.

NERJA & THE CAVES

Nerja, located on the Costa del Sol in southern Spain, is a picturesque town celebrated for its beautiful beaches, whitewashed houses, and charming ambiance. The town has a rich history dating back to the Phoenicians and Romans, with notable landmarks such as the Nerja Caves, discovered in 1959 and considered one of Europe's extensive unexplored cave systems. The beaches in Nerja, including the popular Burriana Beach, Calahonda Beach, Maro Beach, and El Playazo Beach, offer stunning coastal experiences. Besides beach activities, you can explore the historic center, hike in nearby mountains, take a boat trip along the coast, or enjoy various water sports. Nerja boasts a Mediterranean climate that provides warm, dry summers and mild winters, with average temperatures of 28°C (82°F) in July and 15°C (59°F) in January. Whether seeking relaxation or adventure, Nerja stands out as an appealing vacation destination.

GETTING TO NERJA FROM MALAGA

Under favorable traffic conditions, Nerja is a 45 minutes journey from Malaga and can extend to an hour during during peak period. For a more scenic route and a comfortable, air-conditioned travel experience, opting for the Alsa bus line from Maria Zambrano Station, you can arrive in Nerja in just ninety minutes with no intermediate stops. The ticket prices ranges between €5 to €8! Once the bus brings you to Nerja, a brief 10-minute stroll will take you to the city center.

MUST-SEES IN NERJA

Balcony of Europe: A stunning viewpoint offering panoramic views of the Mediterranean. | **Nerja Caves**: A series of impressive caves featuring stalactites and stalagmites. | **Burriana Beach:** One of Nerja's most popular beaches with golden sands and clear waters. | **Church of El Salvador:** A historic church showcasing Mudejar and Gothic architecture. | **Eagle Aqueduct:** A unique structure dating back to the 19th century. | **Maro Beaches:** Explore the secluded coves and crystal-clear waters near the village of Maro. | **Chillar River Walk:** Hike along the scenic Chillar River for a refreshing nature experience. | **Carabeo Beach:** A quieter alternative to the bustling beaches, perfect for relaxation. | **Cala el Cañuelo Beach:** Renowned for its pristine, transparent waters, this secluded cove is an ideal spot to unwind and bask in tranquility. | **Capistrano Playa:** Recognized for its serene waters, this beach is a perfect destination for families with young children seeking a peaceful setting. | **Punta Lara:** A rocky promontory that provides breathtaking coastal views, this location is a favored spot for snorkeling and diving enthusiasts. | **Frigiliana:** Nestled atop a hill, this picturesque village, characterized by its whitewashed buildings, exudes charm and showcases traditional Andalusian architecture.

20 BEST THINGS TO DO IN NERJ

Witness a serene sunrise at Balcón de Europa, offering breathtaking views of the Mediterranean Sea and mountains with fewer crowds. | **Explore Playa Calahonda** Beach near Balcón de Europa, featuring sandy shores, impressive rock formations, and the charming Casa De Don Ducano fisherman's house. | **Capture stunning photos at the White Arches**, Balcón de Europa Square, and treat yourself to ice cream while enjoying panoramic views. | **Stroll through the enchanting Calle Tajillo** in Nerja's Old Town, leading to the Mirador de Calle Tajillo viewpoint. | **Discover the vibrant Rainbow Steps and visit the 'La Dorada' fishing boat**, a significant spot from the TV series "Blue Summer." | **Delight in local tapas** at Restaurante La Piqueta Plaza or Restaurante El Náutico Beach Club, and explore the Saturday market at Plaza de España. | **Admire the Aqueduct Eagle up close**, located a short distance from Nerja's center, showcasing impressive arches on four levels. | **Explore the famous Cueva de Nerja**, a prominent tourist attraction with massive stalagmites and stalactites. | **Embark on a cave tour** at the Nerja Caves, uncovering underground chambers with magnificent rock formations and artifacts. | **Indulge in paella at Playa de Burriana**, the largest beach in Nerja, and visit Ayos or Chiringuito Mauri for a delightful beachside meal. | **Relax at Marro Beach**, one of Andalusia's best beaches, offering crystal-clear waters, stunning rock formations, and waterfalls. | **Experience the Rio Chillar river walk**, a unique summer activity in Nerja, immersing you in nature with knee-deep river waters and natural pools. | **Hike up El Cielo**, the tallest coastal mountain in the region, for breathtaking views of mountains, countryside, and the ocean. | **Visit the Eagle Aqueduct**, Acueducto del Aguila, just outside Nerja, showcasing a fully functional aqueduct from the 1800s. | **Stroll along Balcon de Europa**, central to Nerja, enjoying sea views during the day and vibrant nightlife with festivals and concerts. | **Wander around Nerja's historic center**, featuring narrow streets, old buildings, and landmarks like El Salvador Church and Nuestra Senora de las Angustias Hermitage. | **Dance the night away at Tutti Fruitti Plaza**, Nerja's lively nightlife hub, with dancing, street music, and a vibrant party atmosphere until 4 am. | **Kayak or paddleboard along the Nerja Coast**, exploring hidden coves, sea caves, and secluded beaches. | **Snorkel or dive in Nerja's clear blue waters**, discovering marine life beneath the surface. | **Take a day trip to Frigiliana**, a picturesque town less than 30 minutes away, known as one of Spain's prettiest villages.

12 BEST RESTAURANTS TO DINE IN NERJA

Ayo | Burriana Beach: Ayo's, established in 1969, is a legendary Chiringuito on Burriana Beach, known for its enormous paellas cooked by the owner and chef, Ayo. The lively atmosphere and unforgettable paella make it a must-visit, with the Pollo Asado being another standout dish. | **Copa Vino | Calle Almte. Ferrándiz:** A relatively new addition to Nerja's culinary scene, Copa Vino offers a limited but delicious menu. The warm ambiance, attentive staff, and standout dishes like Penne Piccolo contribute to its growing popularity. | Taste Of India Nerja | **Calle Hernando De Carabeo:** Recognized not only as one of the best in Nerja but also among the finest Indian restaurants, Taste of India stands out for its richly flavored dishes, particularly the Butter Chicken. The attentive staff adds to the overall delightful experience. | **Restaurant 34 Nerja | Calle Hernando De Carabeo, Nº 34:** A sophisticated choice for the last night, Restaurant 34 offers a diverse menu with exquisite views over the Mediterranean Sea. The consistently excellent menu, romantic setting, and the indulgent chocolate fondant make it a highlight. | **Dolores El Chispa | Calle San Pedro:** For an authentic Spanish seafood tapas experience away from the touristy spots, Dolores El Chispa on Calle San Pedro is a must-visit. It's a local gem, offering incredible value, but be prepared for its popularity. | **D'Vinos | Calle Almte. Ferrándiz**: D'Vinos adds a twist to traditional tapas with Japanese and Indian influences. The rooftop terrace provides a great view of the bustling street below, and the fusion of cuisines adds an exciting element to the dining experience. | **Bar El Pulguilla:** A lively tapas restaurant, Bar El Pulguilla, offers an authentic Spanish experience with excellent seafood tapas. The front bar provides a chaotic yet fun atmosphere, while the back has a more extensive menu featuring freshly caught fish. | **Bar Redondo:** Despite some recent inconsistencies, Bar Redondo remains a favorite for its barrel tables, people-watching, and free tapas with each drink. The flaming chorizo is a must-try, even though the tapas quality may vary. | **Restaurante Patanegra 57:** Positioned as a fine dining experience, Patanegra 57, located on Calle Almt. Fernandez, emphasizes locally sourced and seasonal ingredients. While on the pricier side, the culinary delights, especially featuring unique items, make it worthwhile. | **Bakus:** Renowned for its sea views and dreamy sunsets, Bakus offers reliable and creative dishes with bold flavors. The terrace above Playa Carabeillo is particularly popular during the summer months. | **Oliva | Plaza De España:** Established at Plaza de Espana, Oliva is celebrated for its fine dining experience, presenting ambitious flavors inspired by Spanish cuisine. Despite the higher prices, the quality ingredients and creative dishes justify the cost. | **Restaurante Trattoria Italia | C. Almte. Ferrándiz:** A recent favorite, Trattoria Italia, offers delicious and value-for-money meals. The attentive staff, delightful ambience, and standout dishes like steak with potatoes and pasta carbonara make it a repeat-worthy choice.

SOUVENIRS

The majority of Nerja's shops are situated in its charming old quarter, adjacent to the famous Balcony of Europe. These establishments feature a variety of offerings, including pottery, small works of art, beach and everyday attire, accessories, organic and denomination of origin food products, as well as beauty items—ensuring you'll find everything you need for your vacation and unique gifts for loved ones. Below is our curated selection of noteworthy shops and businesses in Nerja, each with its own captivating story. | **EL 8 DE LA CALLE EL BARRIO:** Specializing in handcrafted items by Spanish artisans, this shop offers unique decor pieces, jewelry, and accessories made from materials such as cork, ceramic, stones, and silver. Notable are the owner's folded books, featuring messages creatively displayed on the front edge. | **ARTE DE CORAZÓN:** Owned by Caroline, this store showcases her own creations alongside handmade items by Spanish artisans. Discover signature jewelry, fashion accessories, jeweled buckles for custom-made belts, decoration items, and Native American objects—all chosen or crafted with passion. | **ALWAN:** Meaning "colors" in Arabic, Alwan is a haven for decor items, gifts, jewelry, and home furnishings from Moroccan, Indian, Turkish, and Egyptian origins. Standouts include Empire-style furniture reproductions made in Egypt, adding a touch of cultural richness. | **LA TIENDA DE LA CERÁMICA:** Specializing in artisanal pottery, this shop offers handmade ceramic decoration items and cookware, including fountains, dishes, jugs, and vinegar and oil dispensers. The high-temperature firing makes the pottery suitable for use in ovens and microwaves. | **LAS HIERBAS BUENAS:** A food shop with a focus on quality, Las Hierbas Buenas offers teas, infusions, freshly ground coffee, honey, extra virgin olive oil, chocolate, nuts, and dried fruit. Cookware for preparing and enjoying infusions is also available. | **AZABACHE MODA Y DECORACIÓN:** This shop features casual Spanish brand clothing, accessories, decoration items, and jewelry with semi-precious stones—all handcrafted by the owners. A blend of fashion and decor awaits on calle Carabeo.

STREET MARKETS IN NERJA: **Tuesday Morning Market:** Located at Urbanización Flamingo, this market offers a wide range of items. | **Sunday Flea Market:** Ideal for antique and second-hand enthusiasts, located at Urbanización Flamingo. | **Arts and Crafts Market (June-October):** Found on calle Diputación and Plaza Cangrejo, offering unique handmade crafts.

SHOPPING CENTRES NEAR NERJA: If you prefer larger shopping centers, two options near Nerja are: El Ingenio Shopping Centre | Rincón de la Victoria Shopping Centre

CAMINITO DEL REY

The King's Little Path, known as El Caminito del Rey, is a narrow walkway secured to the steep walls of a gorge in El Chorro, near Ardales in the province of Málaga, Spain. Originally named Camino del Rey (King's Pathway) and locally referred to as el caminito, this walkway was initially constructed in the early 20th century. However, by the early 21st century, it had fallen into a state of disrepair, leading to partial closure for over ten years. After undergoing extensive repairs and renovations lasting four years, it officially reopened in 2015. The pathway gained notoriety as the "world's most dangerous walkway" after experiencing five fatalities in 1999 and 2000.

GETTING TO CAMINITO DEL REY

To get to Caminito del Rey, you'll need to get to the María Zambrano station in Málaga. From there, board the train line headed to El Chorro train station, which typically takes around 50 minutes. Upon arriving at El Chorro Station, situated close to the end of the Caminito del Rey route, you'll then need to utilize the shuttle bus service to reach the beginning of the trail.

TOP MUST-SEE ATTRACTIONS IN CAMINITO DEL REY

Sillón del Rey (King's Chair): A stone chair and table intricately carved into the side of the Conde de Guadalhorce reservoir in Ardales where, in 1921, King Alfonso XIII ceremoniously signed the documents inaugurating the reservoir. | **Desfiladero de los Gaitanes (Gaitanes Gorge):** A narrow gorge situated in the Ardales municipality of Málaga, Spain, renowned for its dramatic cliffs and breathtaking views. | **Mirador de Tres Embalses**

(Three Reservoirs Viewpoint): A scenic viewpoint located in the Ardales municipality of Málaga, Spain, providing panoramic vistas of the Conde de Guadalhorce, Guadalteba, and Guadalhorce reservoirs. | **Puente colgante del Caminito del Rey (Suspension Bridge):** A 100-meter-long suspension bridge spanning the Gaitanes Gorge in Ardales, Spain, originally constructed in 1905 and later restored in 2014. | **Sendero del Gaitanejo (Gaitanejo Trail):** A hiking trail situated in the Ardales municipality of Málaga, Spain, traversing the picturesque Gaitanes Gorge. | **Bobastro Ruins:** The remnants of a Mozarabic settlement dating back to the 9th century, situated in the Ardales municipality of Málaga, Spain. | **Mirador De Las Buitreras (Buitreras Viewpoint):** A viewpoint located in the Ardales municipality of Málaga, Spain, offering sweeping views of the Guadalhorce reservoir and the surrounding mountains. | **Necrópolis de las Aguilillas (Aguilillas Necropolis):** A historical necropolis located in the Ardales municipality of Málaga, Spain, with origins dating back to the 9th and 10th centuries. | **Playa Ardales (Ardales Beach):** A beach situated on the shores of the Conde de Guadalhorce reservoir in Ardales, Spain. | **Pico del Convento (Convent Peak):** A mountain peak located in the Ardales municipality of Málaga, Spain, providing panoramic views of the surrounding landscape. | **Cave of Ardales:** A cave located in the Ardales municipality of Málaga, Spain, renowned for its prehistoric paintings and Paleolithic remains. | **Pantano Del Chorro (Chorro Reservoir):** A reservoir located in the Ardales municipality of Málaga, Spain, formed by the damming of the Guadalhorce River.

THINGS TO DO NEAR EL CAMINITO DEL REY

Excursion to 'Bobastro': Explore the ancient medina of Bobastro. Once a significant military fortress, it now showcases remnants, including a mozarab church and traces of houses. The journey provides insight into the history of rebel leader Omar Ibn Hafsún. | **Hiking in the Surrounding Natural Setting:** Extend your adventure beyond Caminito del Rey with hiking trails in the surrounding natural setting. The diverse landscape, with nearly 150 bird species, offers both challenging routes and accessible trails. The peak of 'Sierra de Huma' at 1,200 meters rewards hikers with breathtaking views. | **Visit to 'Álora':** Discover the charm of Álora, a small town with a rich history. Visit 'El Madrugón' for a taste of local life, explore the castle, and enjoy panoramic views from the 'Ali Ben Falcún Al Baezi' viewpoint.

Álora boasts gastronomic delights, including the unique 'aloreña' olive with Designation of Origin. | **Bath in 'El Chorro':** Refresh yourself at the 'El Chorro' reservoir after exploring the region. The area offers bathing spots, water activities, and recreational areas. Numerous restaurants provide a chance to savor local cuisine, and classic spots like 'El Mirador' and 'El Kiosko' are near the north access to Caminito del Rey. | **Sleep in Paradise:** Experience rural accommodations near Caminito del Rey, such as 'The Olive Brunch,' 'Finca La Campana,' and 'Almona Chica.' 'La Garganta' tourist complex, with 27 rooms and a picturesque pool, offers a serene escape. Enjoy local dishes and artisanal beers and wines with scenic views. | **Discover the Ardales Caves:** Unearth the secrets of the Ardales Caves, discovered after an earthquake in the 19th century. With over 1,500 meters of route and wall paintings dating back 37,000 years, the caves showcase human traces.

GIBRALTAR

Gibraltar is a British Overseas Territory located at the southern tip of the Iberian Peninsula, sharing a border with Spain. Nestled between the Mediterranean Sea and the Atlantic Ocean, Gibraltar is renowned for its iconic landmark, the Rock of Gibraltar. Rising 426 meters above sea level, the Rock offers breathtaking panoramic views of the surrounding areas, including the Strait of Gibraltar and, on clear days, the African continent. The territory holds historical significance, with evidence of human habitation dating back to the Neanderthal era. Over the centuries, Gibraltar has been strategically important due to its location, serving as a military stronghold and a key naval base. Gibraltar is a unique blend of British and Mediterranean influences, evident in its diverse culture, architecture, and cuisine. The town center features charming streets, vibrant markets, and a mix of British and Spanish architectural styles. Notably, Gibraltar is home to a population of Barbary macaques, the only wild monkeys in Europe, adding a touch of natural allure to the area. Tourists often visit Gibraltar for its rich history, stunning vistas, and the opportunity to explore attractions such as St. Michael's Cave, the Moorish Castle, and the Great Siege Tunnels. The territory's strategic location at the entrance to the Mediterranean makes it a fascinating destination, seamlessly blending natural beauty, cultural heritage, and a distinct British identity.

HOW TO GET TO GIBRALTAR

BY CAR: *Driving Time:* Approximately 1.5 to 2 hours, depending on traffic.

Take the AP-7 highway towards Algeciras/Cádiz. Continue onto the A-7 highway, following signs for Algeciras. Once near La Línea de la Concepción, the town closest to Gibraltar, follow signs to the Gibraltar border. Parking is available near the border, and you can walk across. | **BY BUS:** *Bus Service:* There are direct bus services from Malaga to La Línea de la Concepción, the Spanish town near Gibraltar. *Duration:* Approximately 3 hours. From La Línea de la Concepción, you can walk across the border into Gibraltar. | **BY TRAIN AND BUS COMBINATION:** *Train:* Take a train from Malaga to San Roque-La Línea station. *Bus:* From San Roque-La Línea station, take a bus to La Línea de la Concepción. Walk across the border into Gibraltar. | **BY TAXI:** Taxis are available for hire and can take you directly to the Gibraltar border. Confirm the fare with the driver before starting the journey. | **BY ORGANIZED TOURS**: Several tour companies offer day trips from Malaga to Gibraltar, providing transportation and guided tours. This option is convenient for those who prefer a structured itinerary. | **BY RENTAL CAR:** Renting a car in Malaga gives you flexibility and the freedom to explore Gibraltar at your own pace. Ensure the rental car company allows cross-border travel, and familiarize yourself with any additional requirements.

Before traveling, check the latest travel restrictions, as they may vary based on the current situation or regulations. Additionally, have valid identification and travel documents, as Gibraltar is a border territory, and you will need to pass through immigration control.

Part of St Michael's Cave, Gibraltar (image created by Mike McBey)

HOW TO SPEND A DAY IN GIBRALTAR

Covering all attractions in Gibraltar within a single day is challenging. Therefore, I'll outline the key highlights for maximizing your one-day itinerary on a day trip from Malaga to Gibraltar.

TAKE THE CABLE CAR TO THE ROCK'S SUMMIT: Utilize the cable car to reach the top of The Rock swiftly. Operating daily from 09:30 every 10-15 minutes, this 6-minute ride offers spectacular views from vintage cable car wagons dating back to 1966, saving you time compared to climbing the steps. | **ENJOY VIEWS FROM THE ROCK OF GIBRALTAR:** At the summit, 426 meters above sea level, relish breathtaking views of the port, the peninsula, and the Spanish mainland. On clear days, the sight extends to Morocco across the Strait of Gibraltar, presenting a picturesque image of the Spanish coastline. | **CAPTURE MOMENTS WITH GIBRALTAR'S WILD MONKEYS:** Gibraltar is unique for hosting wild monkeys, originating from Morocco. While a major tourist attraction, exercise caution: refrain from feeding them, keep food secure, avoid touching them, watch belongings, and remain calm if approached, as they can bite. | **LUNCH AT MONS CALPE SUITE:** Adjacent to the Cable Car stop, the Mons Calpe Suite offers an ideal lunch spot with panoramic views of The Rock and the Spanish coastline. A convenient choice to save time searching for a restaurant in the town center, they offer a diverse menu of food, snacks, and drinks. | **EXPLORE ST. MICHAEL'S CAVE:** After lunch, venture to St. Michael's Cave, a spectacular natural wonder featuring stalagmites and stalactites formed over millions of years. The cave, open from 09:00 to 19:15 daily, showcases colorful lighting, creating a mesmerizing spectacle. | **VISIT THE MOORISH CASTLE:** Explore Gibraltar's Moorish Castle, initially constructed in the 1100s, destroyed during the Spanish re-conquest, and later rebuilt. The Tower of Homage, along with remnants of fortified walls, stands as a historical gem, offering stunning sea views. | **STROLL AROUND THE TOWN CENTER:** Conclude your day with a leisurely stroll through the town center. Wander down Main Street, home to upscale British shops, snap a photo in a red British phone booth, explore old bookstores, and relax at local bars. Consider a guided tour for insights into Gibraltar's rich history.

FUENGIROLA

This coastal town provides an excellent escape from Malaga, and reaching it is quite convenient. For those with a car, the drive from Malaga to Fuengirola is a mere 30 minutes. Alternatively, you can opt for the bus departing from Malaga bus station, offering several daily departures. The journey takes approximately an hour and costs €3.50. Bus timings can be checked on their official website - *https://booking.avanzabus.com*. ***In my personal experience, the best choice to reach Fuengirola*** is the Malaga suburban train, known as Cercanías. Operating from 5 am to 11:30 pm with departures every 20 minutes, the C1 train takes around 45 minutes to reach Fuengirola. Fuengirola is home to the impressive Sohail Castle, originally built by the Moors in 956 AD. Following extensive renovation and reopening in 2000, the castle has become a cultural hub, hosting events and concerts. Its historic charm invites exploration on foot, adding a touch of history to a day trip to Fuengirola. *The main attraction that draws visitors from Malaga* is the beautiful coastline and pristine beaches. The Paseo Maritimo, a picturesque boardwalk, extends along the 7km stretch of sandy shores. Visitors can enjoy a leisurely walk while taking in the scenic views. Beachside chiringuitos offer an authentic experience with delectable seafood & refreshing beverages.

TOP SIGHTS IN FUENGIROLA

Bioparc Fuengirola: An award-winning animal park featuring over 3,000 animals from 150 species, offering an immersive experience in their natural habitats. | **Castillo Sohail:** An 11th-century Moorish castle situated on a hill, providing free entry and stunning panoramic views of Fuengirola and its coastline. | **Aquamijas:** A water park with an array of slides, pools, and rides suitable for all ages, providing a refreshing escape on hot days. | **Marenostrum Castle Park:** An amusement park in the heart of Fuengirola offering diverse rides, games, and shows for visitors of all ages. | **Playa de los Boliches:** A beach located in Los Boliches, east of Fuengirola, renowned for swimming, sunbathing, and windsurfing. | **Sould Park Fuengirola - Parque infantil y Atracciones:** An amusement park in Fuengirola center, catering to children with various rides, games, and attractions. | **Playa de Fuengirola:** The primary beach in Fuengirola, popular for swimming, sunbathing, and various watersports. | *Playa de San Francisco:* A smaller, less crowded beach just west of Fuengirola, offering a more tranquil seaside experience. | **Playa de Torreblanca:** Located east of Fuengirola, a favored spot for windsurfing and kitesurfing enthusiasts. | **Mercadillo de Fuengirola (Domingo):** A Sunday morning market in Fuengirola center, perfect for finding souvenirs, local produce, and handmade crafts. | **Fuengirola Adventure Golf:** A mini golf course providing family and friends with a fun-filled experience. | **Fuengirola Central Mosque:** The largest mosque in Andalusia, open to the public for tours outside of prayer times. | **Playa de Carvajal:** A beach east of Fuengirola, popular for swimming, sunbathing, and hiking. | **Playa del Ejido:** Situated just east of Fuengirola, a beach attracting visitors for swimming, sunbathing, and fishing.

CORDOBA

Cordoba, a captivating city located just a scenic drive away from Malaga, offers a rich blend of history, culture, and architectural wonders. Known for its mesmerizing Mezquita Cathedral, a UNESCO World Heritage site, Cordoba boasts a unique blend of Moorish and Spanish influences. The historic old town, with its charming cobbled streets and vibrant flower-filled patios, invites exploration. Wander through the Alcazar de los Reyes Cristianos, visit the iconic Bell Tower, and immerse yourself in the city's Arab-Andalusian atmosphere.

GETTING TO CORDOBA

WITH RENTAL CAR: Driving to Cordoba is ideal if you've already rented a car in Malaga. Keep in mind that the Distance between Malaga and Cordoba is 163 km and the journey takes about 2 hours, depending on traffic and route. Leave Malaga early for ample exploration time. Check for toll roads and have cash ready. Plan parking in Cordoba, especially if staying close to the center. | **WITH PUBLIC TRANSPORT:** Affordable and convenient, public transport (train recommended) offers multiple daily connections. Trains depart from Malaga Maria Zambrano station. The journey takes approximately 1 hour and tickets cost range from 23 to 44 euros one way. There are up to 15 connections daily, with the earliest departure from Malaga at 8am and last returning train from Cordoba to Malaga at 10pm. Purchase tickets in advance on the Renfe website. | **WITH TAXI:** The priciest option involves using a taxi, estimated between 150 and 180 euros one way for a standard car (up to 4 people). | **WITH A LOCAL TRAVEL COMPANY:** The hassle-free approach involves using a local travel company, providing several advantages including: Enjoy flexibility with free cancellation up to 24 hours before the trip, and the option to reserve now and pay later. Most packages includes skip-the-line tickets to the Cathedral, a guided tour with insights into its history, a local guide proficient in English and Spanish, a central Malaga pick-up point, comfortable modern air-conditioned bus travel, and availability six times a week.

GETTING AROUND CORDOBA

Navigating Cordoba is straightforward, and there's little necessity for public transportation to discover its attractions. Cordoba is eminently pedestrian-friendly, with key attractions conveniently situated in close proximity. Public transport might only be considered if venturing to the outskirts or neighboring towns. An excellent option for exploring Cordoba is to avail the hop-on hop-off sightseeing bus tour. This tour efficiently transports you around the city, providing audio commentary in English and various languages, along with two guided walking tours.

ACTIVITIES IN CORDOBA FOR A DAY TRIP FROM MALAGA

If you choose to explore Cordoba independently rather than opting for a guided tour, consider this one-day itinerary that covers essential attractions:

VISIT MEZQUITA DE CORDOBA: Explore the iconic Mosque-Cathedral of Cordoba, La Mezquita, a UNESCO World Heritage Site since 1984. Built in 785 during Al-Andalus, it later transformed into a cathedral. The architecture reflects various styles, including Moorish and Renaissance, showcasing the city's diverse history. Allow approximately 2 hours for this visit. | **WALK ON PUENTE ROMANO:** Experience the Roman Bridge of Cordoba, dating back to the 1st century BC. Offering splendid views of the Guadalquivir River and Mezquita, a stroll on Puente Romano is recommended, particularly during sunrise or sunset. Allocate 15-20 minutes for this activity. | **WANDER THE JUDERÍA:** Explore the Jewish Quarter, La Judería, filled with charming alleys, monuments, and museums. Highlights include the Synagogue, Bullfighting Museum, and Andalusian patios in La Casa Andalusi. Enjoy window shopping in the area, with a suggested time of 1 hour or more if visiting museums or monuments. | **TAKE A LOOK AT THE SYNAGOGUE:** While in the Jewish

Quarter, don't miss the Synagogue of Cordoba, one of Andalusia's best-preserved synagogues. Its Mudejar architectural style and a small decorated patio make it a worthwhile visit, taking approximately 15-20 minutes. | **LUNCH AT TABERNA EL CAPRICHO:** Dine at Taberna el Capricho, a restaurant close to Calleja de las Flores, offering affordable tapas or a set menu. Popular for dishes like rabo de toro (oxtail stew), the set menu includes a starter, main course, dessert, bread, and a drink. Spend as much time as desired. | **TAKE PHOTOS AT CALLEJA DE LAS FLORES:** Capture the beauty of Calleja de las Flores, the most picturesque street in Cordoba, located in the Jewish Quarter. Admire the narrow street with whitewashed buildings adorned with flower pots. The time spent depends on whether you choose to walk or take photos. | **ALCAZAR DE LOS REYES CRISTIANOS:** Explore the Alcazar of the Christian Monarchs, a UNESCO World Heritage fortress located a few minutes from Mezquita and Puente Romano. Immerse yourself in history while wandering through beautifully manicured gardens with fountains, courtyards, and Mudejar architecture. Plan for approximately 2 hours. | **VISIT PALACIO DE VIANA:** Head to Palacio de Viana, a Renaissance palace known for its Andalusian courtyards. With over 10 unique patios open year-round, it provides insights into Roman and Muslim traditions. Allocate 1 to 1.5 hours for this visit. | **VISIT TO CÓRDOBA HAMMAM AL ÁNDALUS:** Córdoba Hammam Al Ándalus offers a luxurious experience, allowing you to indulge in steam rooms, cold and warm baths, and a soothing massage to pamper yourself.

TIPS FOR A DAY TRIP FROM MALAGA TO CORDOBA

AVOID SUMMER MONTHS: It's advisable not to visit Cordoba during the summer months when temperatures soar above 40 degrees Celsius. The extreme heat can make sightseeing challenging, hindering the exploration of the city's offerings. | **EXPLORE ANDALUSIAN COURTYARDS:** One of the compelling reasons to visit Cordoba is to explore its Andalusian courtyards. Spring is the optimal time for this experience, as all courtyards are open, and the blossoming flowers enhance their beauty. Certain patios, such as Palacio de Viana, remain accessible throughout the year. | **INDULGE IN TRADITIONAL DISHES:** Delight your taste buds by ordering traditional Cordoban dishes at local restaurants. Try specialties like flamenquín (pork loin coated in breadcrumbs, stuffed with ham and cheese), salmorejo (a cold tomato soup with ham and hard-boiled egg), and rabo de toro (oxtail stew).

| **CONSIDER A LONGER STAY:** While it's possible to cover Cordoba's main attractions in a day, extending your stay allows for exploration of nearby places such as Medina Azahara or charming towns like Iznajar or Rute.

Embarking on a day trip from Malaga to Cordoba is undoubtedly worthwhile. Beyond its proximity to Malaga, Cordoba boasts remarkable historical buildings, enchanting Andalusian patios, and delectable traditional cuisine.

SEVILLE

Seville is the capital and largest city of the Spanish autonomous community of Andalusia. It is situated on the lower reaches of the River Guadalquivir in the southwest of the Iberian Peninsula. As of 2022, it has a municipal population of about 701,000 and a metropolitan population of approximately 1.5 million. Recognized for its historical significance, the old town of Seville, covering 4 square kilometers, includes a UNESCO World Heritage Site featuring the Alcázar palace complex, the Cathedral, and the General Archive of the Indies. Seville was once a prominent hub of Moorish rule - The iconic Giralda Tower, originally constructed as a minaret, stands tall as a testament to the city's Islamic past. As you venture from Malaga to Seville, the picturesque Guadalquivir River, which meanders through the heart of the city, becomes a silent witness to centuries of cultural evolution. Seville's heritage unfolds in its narrow streets, charming squares, and historic neighborhoods, each narrating a unique chapter in the city's story. Beyond its Moorish legacy, Seville boasts a blend of influences, including Gothic, Renaissance, and Baroque, showcased in its architectural wonders. The Alcazar of Seville, a palace complex with stunning Mudejar and Gothic elements, reflects the city's transition under various rulers. This journey from Malaga to Seville promises not just a geographical transition but a cultural odyssey, offering glimpses of a city that has played a pivotal role in shaping Spain's rich historical tapestry.

GETTING TO SEVILLE FROM MALAGA

BY BUS: Direct buses operated by ALSA run from Estación de Autobuses de Málaga to Seville Plaza De Armas. The journey takes approximately two hours and forty-five minutes, with varying prices ranging from €14 to €19. There are ten daily buses, starting from 07:00 and ending at 19:30. | **BY TRAIN:** The train, a faster but relatively more expensive alternative, departs from Malaga Maria Zambrano station and arrives at any of Seville's three train stations, including the main Santa Justa station. The shortest train ride by Renfe is one hour and fifty-five minutes, starting at €37.50 (one-way). There are ten daily trains, with the earliest departing at 06:30 and the latest at 20:15. | **BY CAR**: For those preferring flexibility, the 125-mile (206 kilometers) drive from Malaga to Seville via the A45 and A92 highways takes approximately two hours and fifteen minutes. Renting a car allows control over the schedule and the opportunity to stop for photos. However, it necessitates a designated driver if planning to indulge in sangria or cervezas during the trip.

HOW TO MAKE THE MOST OF A DAY IN SEVILLE

REAL ALCAZAR: A must-visit on your day trip from Malaga to Seville, the Réal Alcazar, a UNESCO World Heritage Site, originally built for King Peter of Castille on a Muslim stronghold, is still a royal residence. Explore ornate tiled rooms, towers, and immaculate gardens. Highlights include the Salon de Embajadores and the Princess Bath. Booking tickets in advance or opting for skip-the-line tours is recommended. | **SEVILLE CATHEDRAL:** As the largest Gothic cathedral globally and a UNESCO World Heritage Site, Seville Cathedral is a cultural and architectural marvel. Admire the sanctuary, intricate Spanish paintings, and religious artifacts. The cathedral houses the remains of Christopher and Diego Columbus. Secure tickets in advance to avoid queues. | **PLAZA DE ESPAÑA:** Constructed in the early 20th century, Plaza de España is an iconic Seville landmark representing Spain's ancient kingdoms and regions. With Venetian-style bridges and vibrant, tiled alcoves, it's a work of art displaying the country's heritage. The plaza, used in films like Star Wars and Game of Thrones, houses governmental facilities. | **FLAMENCO SHOW:** While traditionally a nighttime activity, catching a Flamenco show in Triana, known for authenticity, adds a cultural touch to your day trip. Lola's in Triana offers an unassuming yet authentic venue. Tours or night-out packages including Flamenco performances are available. | **METROPOL PARASOL:** Known as 'las setas' (the mushrooms), the Metropol

Parasol is a distinctive landmark with wooden panels, offering panoramic views. Climbing the structure provides excellent photo opportunities and vistas for €3, including a free drink. | **MARIA LUISA PARK:** The expansive Maria Luisa Park, created for the 1929 Exposición Iberoamericana, offers palm-lined avenues, shaded walkways, and beautiful mosaics. Stroll through the park, visit pavilions serving as museums, and consider renting a bike for an active exploration. | **TRIANA:** The authentic neighborhood of Triana, across the Guadalquivir river, maintains its charm. Known for Flamenco shows, ceramic arts, and the Mercado de Triana, it offers a taste of local life. Explore Castillo de San Jorge beneath the market. | **TAPAS EXPLORATION:** With hundreds of tapas bars, Seville offers a culinary delight. El Rinconcillo, the oldest tapas bar, and La Brunilda for ham croquettes are recommended. Eslava provides creative takes on authentic dishes. Consider a tapas tour for a diverse culinary experience. | **BARRIO SANTA CRUZ:** Seville's Jewish Quarter, Barrio Santa Cruz, with flowered balconies and whitewashed buildings, is a photographer's dream. Wander through the narrow streets, visit Las Columnas for a famous shrimp omelet. | **PALACIO DE LAS DUEÑAS:** Adjacent to the Old Town, Palacio de las Dueñas is an under-visited palace known for its beauty. Explore the grounds and marvel at the palace walls. Spring visits offer blooming flowers for picturesque moments. | **CASA DE PILATOS:** An underrated attraction, Casa de Pilatos, a residence of the Duke of Medinaceli, features impeccable grounds and a charming marble courtyard. Purchase tickets for guided tours and take advantage of free entry hours for EU passport holders on Wednesday afternoons. | **ALCAZAR OF SEVILLE (ROYAL ALCAZAR):** A masterpiece of Mudejar, Renaissance, and Gothic architecture, the Alcazar of Seville, or Royal Alcazar, stands as a testament to centuries of cultural influences. Originally constructed as a fortress by the Moors, it evolved into a palace for Christian monarchs. Explore its intricate courtyards, opulent halls, and lush gardens. The Patio de las Doncellas and the Hall of Ambassadors are architectural marvels. | **GIRALDA TOWER:** Adjacent to the Seville Cathedral, the Giralda Tower is a symbol of the city. Originally built as a minaret during Muslim rule, it later became the cathedral's bell tower. Climb to the top for panoramic views of Seville. The ascent involves a series of ramps, providing a unique experience. | **BARRIO SANTA CRUZ:** Seville's historic Jewish quarter, Barrio Santa Cruz, offers a labyrinth of narrow streets, adorned with colorful flowers and charming squares. Lose yourself in the enchanting atmosphere, discovering hidden plazas and glimpses of Seville's rich history. | **PLAZA DE ESPAÑA:** A stunning example of Renaissance Revival architecture, Plaza de España is a grand semi-circular building with a canal, bridges, and a series of tiled alcoves representing different Spanish provinces. Stroll along the canal, admire the intricate tiles, and appreciate the artistic representation of Spain's regions. | **METROPOL PARASOL (LAS SETAS):** Modern and innovative, the Metropol Parasol, affectionately known as "Las Setas" (the mushrooms), is a wooden structure providing shade to the square below. Ascend to the top for panoramic views of Seville. The intertwining parasols create a striking contrast with the historic surroundings. | **FLAMENCO IN TRIANA:** Triana, known for its deep connection to Flamenco, offers authentic experiences of this passionate and expressive art form. Explore the vibrant streets, discover local Flamenco bars, and immerse yourself in the rhythmic melodies and soulful dances that define Flamenco. | **SEVILLE'S CULINARY DELIGHTS:** Indulge in Seville's culinary scene by sampling traditional tapas. Head to bustling markets like Mercado Lonja del Barranco or Mercado de Triana to savor local flavors. From Iberian ham to salmorejo (a cold tomato soup), Seville's gastronomy is a journey of taste. | **SEVILLE'S FESTIVALS AND TRADITIONS:** Depending on the time of your visit, you might encounter Seville's vibrant festivals. The Semana Santa (Holy Week) processions and the Feria de Abril, a lively spring fair, showcase Seville's rich cultural and religious traditions. Participate in the festivities to experience the city's lively spirit.

A day in Seville is a captivating journey through history, art, and culture. Whether you explore its architectural wonders, savor its culinary delights, or immerse yourself in the rhythms of Flamenco, Seville leaves an indelible mark on every visitor. As the sun sets over the Guadalquivir, the enchanting ambiance of Seville lingers, inviting you to return and delve deeper into its timeless allure.

GRANADA

Granada is the capital city of the province of Granada, situated in the autonomous community of Andalusia, Spain. Nestled at the base of the Sierra Nevada mountains, where the Darro, Genil, Monachil, and Beiro rivers converge, Granada boasts an average elevation of 738 meters (2,421 feet) above sea level. Despite its mountainous setting, the city is conveniently located just an hour's drive from the Mediterranean coast, known as the Costa Tropical. Additionally, the Sierra Nevada Ski Station, host to the FIS Alpine World Ski Championships in 1996, is in close proximity. As of the 2021 national census, the city of Granada proper had a population of 227,383, while the entire municipal area was estimated at 231,775 inhabitants, making it the 20th-largest urban area in Spain. The city's nearest airport is the Federico García Lorca Granada-Jaén Airport. Granada has a rich history, with settlements dating back to ancient times, including periods of Iberian, Roman, and Visigothic influence. It rose to prominence during the 11th century as a major city in Al-Andalus under the Zirid Taifa of Granada. In the 13th century, it became the capital of the Emirate of Granada during Nasrid rule, marking the final Muslim-ruled state in the Iberian Peninsula. The Catholic Monarchs conquered Granada in 1492, initiating its transformation into a Christian city throughout the 16th century. A standout architectural marvel in Granada is the Alhambra, a medieval Nasrid citadel and palace celebrated for its Islamic architecture. It stands as one of the most renowned monuments of its kind and ranks among the top tourist sites in Spain.

The influence of Islamic and Moorish architecture extends to the Albaicín neighborhood and other medieval structures in the city. The 16th century witnessed a flourishing of Mudéjar and Renaissance architecture, succeeded by Baroque and Churrigueresque styles.

GETTING TO GRANADA FROM MALAGA

BY CAR: The quickest route, taking approximately one hour and twenty minutes, is driving, but this requires having a personal vehicle. If time efficiency is a priority and you have a rental car, this can be an ideal choice, allowing you to depart at your convenience and avoid crowds at the Alhambra. | **BY BUS:** If you are on a budget, taking the bus is the most economical option, with fares ranging from $10 to $14. Avanzo Grupo operates four daily services from Malaga to Granada, with a travel time of less than two hours. | **BY TRAIN:** On the other hand, the train presents the longest and priciest journey. Involving a transfer, the total train duration is around two hours and fifteen minutes. Commence the journey at Malaga Maria Zambrano station, taking a train to Antequera-Santa Ana, followed by another train to Granada. While train tickets can be as low as $20 USD, the actual cost, depending on the chosen time and date, is more realistically around $55 USD for a one-way ticket. This option can become considerably expensive, especially when considering return tickets for multiple travelers. | Given these considerations, the bus is recommended for its cost-effectiveness, or, if you have your vehicle, driving provides a quick and flexible alternative for a day trip from Malaga to Granada.

EXPLORING GRANADA IN A DAY

DISCOVER THE ALHAMBRA: Immerse yourself in the world-renowned Alhambra, a must-visit site in Spain. Originating in the late 800s as a small fortress on Roman ruins, the Alhambra transformed into the Nasrid rulers' residence and summer retreat in the 1300s. After the Reconquista in the 1400s, Ferdinand and Isabella enhanced the palace, with top attractions including the Alcazaba, Charles V Palace, and the exquisite Nasrid Palace, showcasing intricate Moorish architecture. A UNESCO World Heritage Site since 1984, booking tickets well in advance is essential. | **SEEK SHADE IN GENERALIFE GARDENS:** Explore the Generalife gardens, an enchanting retreat adjacent to the Alhambra. Once a haven for Nasrid rulers, these lush gardens feature tiered fountains, manicured topiaries, and reflection pools, offering respite from the summer heat. Comparable to Versailles, the Generalife gardens provide a serene contrast to the grandeur of the Alhambra. | **GRANADA CATHEDRAL:** Visit the Granada Cathedral, Spain's second-largest and the world's fourth-largest cathedral. Dominating Granada's historic center, this 16th-century marvel blends Baroque and Renaissance styles. While unfinished, it boasts stunning stained glass windows, a grand altar, and numerous side chapels. Entrance costs €5 and includes an audio guide, available for exploration on weekdays. | **ROYAL**

CHAPEL: A short stroll from Granada Cathedral leads to the Royal Chapel, the resting place of monarchs Ferdinand and Isabella. Commissioned by the royal couple in the early 16th century, it also houses successors Joanna of Castile and Philip I. Admire the alabaster tomb's aesthetics, although the rulers are interred in the crypt below. Entrance allows exploration of this historical site. | **PLAZA DE BIB RAMBLA:** Relax in Plaza de Bib Rambla, a picturesque square near Granada Cathedral. Lined with restaurants, bars, and shops, it offers the ideal spot for people-watching. Enjoy an outdoor table under the shade of trees and unwind from your day trip, especially during the warmer months. | **EXPLORE ALBAYZÍN, GRANADA'S ARAB QUARTER:** Wander through Albayzín, Granada's Arab Quarter, recognized as a UNESCO World Heritage Site. Settled by the Moorish population after the Reconquista, it captivates with its architecture and Moorish tiles. Its labyrinthine streets, resembling a Medina, house tapas bars, cafes, and the Mirador San Nicolas, providing stunning views of the Alhambra. | **VISIT ALCAICERIA FOR SOUVENIRS:** Discover Alcaiceria, once Granada's Grand Bazaar during Moorish rule. Presently a narrow alley filled with souvenir shops, it offers hand-painted Moorish ceramics and intricately carved wood items. Haggling may secure better prices, and even without purchasing, it provides an enjoyable stroll. | **EXPLORE SACROMONTE NEIGHBORHOOD:** Explore Sacromonte, east of Albayzín, known for its Roma (gypsy) population and distinctive cave homes. The unique architecture results from the terrain, and the neighborhood hosts vibrant flamenco performances, making a night tour a worthwhile consideration if your schedule allows. | **VISIT THE BAÑUELO:** Explore the Arab baths on Carrera del Darro, surviving remnants from Moorish times. Free to visit, these baths offer a glimpse into an authentic hammam, adorned with Roman-era columns. Capture captivating photographs with star-shaped holes in the ceilings, creating mesmerizing light effects. | **MONASTERIO DE SAN JERÓNIMO:** Visit the 16th-century Monasterio de San Jerónimo, the first monastery constructed post-Reconquista. Admire the ornate exterior and vibrant courtyard, fragrant with orange trees. Entrance costs €4, with guided tours available on Sundays after the traditional mass. | **GRANADA CHARTERHOUSE:** Conclude your day at the Granada Charterhouse, a Baroque masterpiece requiring over 300 years to complete. Marvel at Doric columns in the courtyard and rooms adorned with depictions of martyrs. It stands as one of Spain's premier examples of Baroque architecture.

WHERE TO EAT IN GRANADA

You can indulge in delicious tapas, cafes, and restaurants in Granada at the following recommended spots: _Bar Avila on Veronica de la Virgen_, _Bar La Buena Vida on Almiceros_, and _Bodega Legado Andalusi_ for a delightful culinary experience.

MIJAS PUEBLO

Mijas Pueblo stands as the historical nucleus of the Mijas municipality, centrally located in the Costa del Sol region in southwestern Spain, just 30 kilometers from Málaga Airport. Positioned amidst a diverse landscape, the area encompasses mountains extending to the sea. The Mijas region is predominantly mountainous, witnessing ongoing developments along the coastline and on the milder sections of the mountain slopes. The Pasadas and Ojen rivers traverse the region, converging to create the Rio Fuengirola, which ultimately meets the sea near the border of Fuengirola and Mijas. As one of the largest municipalities in the Province of Málaga, spanning 147 km^2, Mijas is divided into three distinct urban zones: Mijas Pueblo, retaining the allure of a traditional Andalusian "white village"; Las Lagunas on the coast, characterized as the most contemporary area with industrial and commercial sectors; and La Cala, a compact yet rapidly expanding coastal village at the heart of the 12-kilometer stretch of beaches along the Mijas coast. Inhabited since ancient times, the small village of Mijas was primarily dedicated to agriculture and fishing until the surge in tourism during the 1950s. Subsequently, tourism and the construction sector have propelled the local economy, simultaneously driving population growth and per capita income, albeit with a notable environmental impact. Presently, Mijas stands as a multicultural city, boasting a significant percentage of residents of foreign origin, and serves as a prominent residential hub for tourism in Andalusia.

GETTING TO MIJAS PUEBLO FROM MALAGA

When traveling from Malaga to Mijas, you have several transportation choices catering to your preferences and budget. Here are the most common methods:

TAXI: Opting for a taxi is the most convenient but also the priciest alternative. Taxis are easily accessible at Malaga Airport and throughout the city. The journey to Mijas typically takes around 30-40 minutes, depending on traffic conditions. | **RENTAL CAR:** For those seeking independence and flexibility, renting a car at Malaga Airport or within the city is an option. Follow the signs for the A-7 or AP-7 highway (toll road) and take exit 214 to reach Mijas. This choice not only facilitates travel to Mijas but also allows exploration of the surrounding areas. | **BUS:** Avanza, the local bus company, operates a service from Malaga to Mijas. Catch the bus at the Malaga Bus Station (Estación de Autobuses) situated near the city center. The journey typically spans 40-50 minutes. | **TRAIN AND BUS:** An alternative involves taking the C-1 Cercanías train from Malaga to Fuengirola, followed by transferring to a bus heading to Mijas. The train journey lasts around 35 minutes, while the bus ride to Mijas takes approximately 15 minutes. Verify train and bus schedules in advance. | **AIRPORT TRANSFER SERVICE**: If you're landing at Malaga Airport, pre-booking an airport transfer service offers convenience and comfort. A driver will meet you at the airport and transport you directly to your destination in Mijas.

TOP ATTRACTIONS AND ACTIVITIES IN MIJAS PUEBLO

Mijas Pueblo (Mijas Village): Explore the charming white-washed village of Mijas Pueblo. Wander through narrow cobblestone streets, appreciate the traditional Andalusian architecture, and visit quaint shops and boutiques. Don't overlook the Plaza de la Constitución with its vibrant flower pots and the breathtaking views from the Mirador de Mijas viewpoint. | **Mijas Donkey Taxi:** Experience a ride on the renowned Mijas Donkey Taxis. Originally used as a mode of transportation in the village, these donkeys now offer a unique and enjoyable way to discover Mijas Pueblo. | **Fuengirola Beach:** Enjoy the proximity to Fuengirola, a coastal town renowned for its beautiful sandy beaches. Spend a day unwinding on the shores, partake in swimming, or try water sports such as jet-skiing and paddleboarding. | **Bioparc Fuengirola:** Explore the innovative zoo in Fuengirola, Bioparc Fuengirola, which prioritizes providing a natural and immersive environment for animals. It's an excellent spot to observe a diverse range of wildlife in an ethical setting. | **Mijas Water Park:** If you're traveling with children or simply enjoy water parks, consider a visit to Mijas Water Park (Aqualand Mijas), featuring water slides, pools, and attractions for all age groups. | **Golf:** Make the most of the Costa del Sol's golfing reputation at courses like Mijas Golf Club and Santana Golf & Country Club, where scenic views accompany a round of golf. | **Casa Museo de Mijas (Mijas Museum):** Immerse yourself in the history and culture of Mijas through its local museum, housed in a beautiful historic building that offers insights into the town's past. | **Hiking and Nature:** Explore the stunning natural landscapes surrounding Mijas, with options for hiking in the nearby Sierra de Mijas or discovering the countryside on horseback. | **Flamenco Shows:** Indulge in an authentic Flamenco show at one of the local restaurants or venues. Flamenco, integral to Andalusian culture, promises a memorable live performance. | **Wine Tasting:** Discover the region's excellent wines through a wine tour, exploring local wineries and savoring the diverse flavors of Spanish wines. | **Mijas Bullring:** Visit the iconic Mijas Bullring, even if not attending a bullfight, to learn about its history and significance. | **Botanical Gardens of Mijas:** If you have an appreciation for gardens and plant life, explore the Cactus and Succulent Gardens in Mijas, featuring a unique collection from around the world.

Fantastic Dining Spots in the Vicinity of Mijas

EXCEPTIONAL DINING SPOTS TO EAT IN MIJAS PUEBLO

If you find yourself hungry and eager to indulge, there are numerous excellent dining options around Mijas, whether you prefer the beachside areas or the charming old town section. Mijas presents a delightful array of dining choices, spanning from authentic Spanish dishes to international flavors. Here are some exceptional places to dine in and around Mijas:

Restaurante El Mirlo Blanco: Positioned in Mijas Pueblo, this establishment boasts a charming terrace with sweeping coastal views. The menu features a blend of Spanish and Mediterranean cuisine, including specialties like paella and fresh seafood. | **Restaurante Valparaiso:** Nestled in the hills above Mijas, Valparaiso is renowned for its picturesque setting and romantic ambiance. Offering a mix of international and Spanish cuisine, the restaurant frequently hosts live music. | **Mesón de Calahonda:** Just a short drive from

Mijas, this traditional Spanish restaurant is celebrated for its grilled meats, particularly succulent steaks. The rustic setting enhances the overall dining experience. | **El Higuerón:** Situated in the Higuerón Hotel, this Michelin-starred restaurant provides a gourmet journey with a modern Mediterranean menu. Expect visually stunning and delicious culinary creations. | **La Alcazaba:** Found in Fuengirola, La Alcazaba is a well-regarded seafood restaurant offering fresh fish dishes in a charming Andalusian ambiance. | **La Luna Blanca:** A popular choice in La Cala de Mijas, this restaurant specializes in Mediterranean cuisine. Enjoy dishes like seafood paella and grilled meats on their terrace overlooking the sea. | **Restaurante El Jinete:** Located near Mijas Pueblo, this family-run restaurant is recognized for its traditional Spanish cuisine and welcoming atmosphere. The menu includes classics such as gazpacho, Iberian ham, and grilled sardines. | **Restaurante Los Marinos José:** In the coastal town of Fuengirola, this seafood restaurant is renowned for its fresh seafood and exceptional service. The menu offers a variety of seafood paellas and grilled fish. | **Tapeo de Cervantes:** Situated in La Cala de Mijas, this tapas bar provides a diverse selection of traditional Spanish tapas, from patatas bravas to jamón ibérico, in a lively and friendly atmosphere. | **Restaurante Avanto:** Within the Higuerón Hotel, Avanto is celebrated for its creative cuisine. Tasting menus showcase locally sourced ingredients and innovative culinary techniques. | **Restaurant Guru:** This restaurant in Mijas Pueblo offers a diverse menu, including vegetarian and vegan options. The terrace provides lovely views of the surrounding area. | **Taberna Flamenca Pepe Lopez:** For an authentic Andalusian experience, consider visiting this tapas bar in Mijas Pueblo. Enjoy live Flamenco music and dance performances while savoring traditional Spanish tapas.

BEST TIME TO VISIT MIJAS PUEBLO

Summer is perfect for those who love beaches and water sports. | **Spring and Early Autumn** provide pleasant weather, ideal for outdoor activities and sightseeing, with fewer tourists around. | **Winter** is a suitable choice for travelers seeking a quieter pace to explore Mijas, along with the benefit of lower prices.

ANTEQUERA

Antequera is a city Known as "the heart of Andalusia" due to its central location among Málaga, Granada, Córdoba, and Seville. It is home to the UNESCO World Heritage site, the *Antequera Dolmens*. With a population of 41,854 in 2011, it covers an area of 749.34 km2, making it the most populous city in the interior of the province and the twenty-second largest in Spain. Situated at an altitude of 575 meters, Antequera is well-connected by high-speed train and the A-45 motorway to Málaga and Córdoba. The city is strategically positioned for transportation logistics, featuring industrial parks and the new Logistics Centre of Andalusia. The fertile Vega de Antequera, irrigated by the river Guadalhorce, is an essential agricultural area producing cereals, olive oil, and vegetables. The nearby natural reserve of El Torcal, famous for its unique limestone rocks, showcases one of Europe's significant karst landscapes. Antequera boasts an extensive archaeological and architectural heritage, including the dolmens of Menga, Viera, and El Romeral, along with various churches, convents, and palaces.

GETTING TO ANTEQUERA

BY TRAIN: Antequera is located just 57km north of Malaga, and you can reach it in a quick 20-minute train ride. The earliest train departs at 6:37 am, taking an hour. For a slightly higher fare, the 7:01 am train shortens the journey to 21 minutes, arriving before the early train. The last train back to Malaga departs at 11 pm, but the 9:57 pm train offers a more economical option, costing about 1/5th of the price. A roundtrip ticket is approximately 15€. |

BY CAR: If you opt for a car rental during your stay in Malaga, the journey to Antequera takes approximately 1 hour. While the train is cost-effective, renting a car may be more practical, especially for larger groups. **BY BUS:** Public buses operate regularly between Malaga and Antequera throughout the day. The earliest bus departs Malaga at 7:45 am, reaching Antequera in just 50 minutes. The last bus from Antequera to Malaga leaves at 7:10 pm, arriving back in Malaga at 8:00 pm. The total cost for a roundtrip bus ticket is 13.10€. | **GUIDED TOUR:** Half-day tours from Malaga to Antequera's UNESCO sites are available. The VIP Antequera Torcal Hiking and Dolmens Site tour includes a 3km hike in El Torcal Natural Park and exploration of the Dolmen Site, excluding the town of Antequera. The Antequera Walking Tour covers all major sites in the town but excludes the Dolmens Site and El Torcal Park.

TIPS FOR YOUR DAY TRIP TO ANTEQUERA

Antequera is small enough to be explored on foot, but be sure to check the opening hours of the places you plan to visit. | If time permits, consider a short trip to Lovers' Rock, an intriguing natural formation associated with local legends and folklore.

21 TOP ATTRACTIONS TO SEE IN ANTEQUERA

Caminito del Rey - North Access: A renowned hiking area with offering breathtaking views. | **El Torcal de Antequera:** A national reserve Known for its unique karst formations, it's an ideal location for hiking and climbing. | **Dolmen de Menga:** A historical landmark featuring one of the largest and best-preserved dolmens in Europe. | **Archaeological Dolmens of Antequera**: An archaeological museum and a UNESCO World Heritage Site, showcasing three dolmens: Menga, Viera, and Tholos de El Romeral. **Lobo Park, Antequera:** An

Torcal de Antequera - image creator & Copyright owner - Miguel Ossorio

animal park home to over 200 wolves, providing educational insights into wolf ecosystems. | **Alcazaba:** A historical landmark, a Moorish fortress offering stunning city and countryside views. | **Peña de los Enamorados:** A mountain peak named after a romantic legend, making it a popular spot for hiking and climbing. | **Tholos de El Romeral:** A historical landmark with a rating of 4.6 (1.4K reviews), a megalithic tomb estimated to be over 5,000 years old. | **Dolmen de Viera:** A historical landmark with a rating of 4.5 (213 reviews), a megalithic tomb estimated to be over 4,000 years old. | **Real Colegiata de Santa María la Mayor:** A Catholic church & a 16th-century Renaissance building housing important works of art. | **Museo de la Ciudad de Antequera (MVCA):** A museum located in a 16th-century palace, exhibiting artifacts showcasing the city's history. | **Guadalmedin** - A river flowing through Antequera, serving as a popular spot for activities such as swimming, fishing, and boating. | **Astronomical Observatory Torcal:** An astronomical observatory, one of the most important in Spain, equipped with various telescopes, including a 1-meter telescope. | **Nacimiento del Río de la Villa:** A nature reserve in Antequera, providing a natural and serene environment. | **Arco de los Gigantes:** is a Roman triumphal arch representing one of the city's remaining Roman structures. Constructed around the 1st century AD, this arch served as an entrance to the city. | **Convento de la Encarnación:** is a former convent in Antequera, dates back to the 16th century and has been repurposed into a museum. Within its walls, you can explore a diverse collection of art, including paintings and sculptures. | **Museo Taurino de Antequera:** is a bullfighting museum showcasing a range of artifacts tied to Spain's bullfighting history. Housed in a 17th-century palace, the museum provides insight into the cultural significance of this tradition. | **Plaza de Toros:** is an 18th-century bullring in Antequera, remains an active venue for bullfighting events. As one of the largest bullrings in Andalusia, it reflects the enduring cultural importance of this traditional spectacle. | **Palacio de los Marqueses de Villadarias:** is a 17th-century palace in has been transformed into a hotel. Its architectural grandeur showcases the Baroque style, contributing to the city's cultural and historical richness. | **Iglesia del Carmen:** Built in the 17th century, the Iglesia del Carmen is a church in Antequera dedicated to Our Lady of Mount Carmel. This religious site houses significant art pieces, including a notable painting by Zurbarán. | **Museo Conventual de las Descalzas:** is situated in a former convent, is now a museum in Antequera. Displaying religious art, the museum features an array of sculptures and paintings, offering visitors a glimpse into the city's cultural and religious heritage.

RESOURCES FOR DAY TRIPS FROM MALAGA

TRAIN RESERVATIONS: If you are opting for a day trip from Malaga by train, it's advisable to secure your train tickets online. Visit the Renfe website at *https://www.renfe.com/es/en* to make your reservations. | **BUS RESERVATIONS:** Planning a day trip from Malaga via bus is both convenient and budget-friendly. The Alsa website at ***https://www.movelia.es/en/area-agencias/home*** serves as a platform for purchasing bus tickets in Spain. Additionally, you can explore the Avanza Bus website at *https://www.avanzabus.com* for alternative options and compare prices, considering the availability of different bus companies. | **CAR RENTAL:** Opting for a day trip from Malaga by car provides the flexibility to explore at your own pace. Discover Cars *(https://www.discovercars.com)*, a car rental service, facilitates a comparison of prices across various rental companies, ensuring you secure the most economical rate. | **GUIDED TOURS:** Numerous day tours from Malaga to neighboring towns are available. Viator (*https://www.viator.com*) and Get Your Guide (*https://www.getyourguide.com*) are reputable companies through which you can book diverse and well-curated tours catering to different interests and preferences.

CHAPTER 11: PRACTICAL INFORMATION & TIPS

STAYING SAFE IN MALAGA

Malaga is a secure destination with a safety score of 76 according to the Travel Safe Abroad Index (*https://www.travelsafe-abroad.com/spain/malaga*).. It's among the safest cities, attracting millions of visitors who explore its attractions without safety concerns. Violent crimes are rare, and there are no major natural disasters to worry about. Nighttime strolls are safe, allowing visitors to enjoy the vibrant nightlife. While Malaga is generally safe, it's essential to stay vigilant. Conducting additional safety research before your trip and checking government travel advisories is wise for all travelers.

COMMON PETTY CRIMES AND SCAMS AFFECTING TOURISTS IN MALAGA

Unlisted Prices: Exercise caution when encountering eateries in Malaga that fail to display prices on their menus. Such establishments may overcharge unsuspecting patrons. Even seemingly modest restaurants might charge more than expected, particularly if they offer daily specials not listed on the menu. | **Petition and Financial Aid Scams:** Beware of locals soliciting signatures for purported charitable causes, as these petitions may be part of a scam. Refrain from making donations, even if pressured to do so. Additionally, be cautious of individuals directly requesting financial assistance for various reasons, as these encounters often turn out to be scams aimed at exploiting the goodwill of tourists. | **Pickpocketing:** While pickpocketing incidents occur sporadically in Malaga despite its sizable population, they are not widespread. Nonetheless, it's advisable to remain vigilant, particularly in crowded areas, to minimize the risk of falling victim to opportunistic thieves.

EMERGENCY CONTACT INFORMATION

Being ready for any unforeseen circumstances is crucial when traveling. Therefore, as you plan your trip to Malaga, it's vital to familiarize yourself with essential emergency numbers. Additionally, ensure you have your embassy's contact information readily available throughout your journey.

- ⇒ Country Code for Spain: +34
- ⇒ Malaga Area Code: +34-95
- ⇒ Emergency Services: 112
- ⇒ National Police: 091
- ⇒ Local Police: 092
- ⇒ Guardia Civil: 062
- ⇒ Ambulance Services: 061
- ⇒ Fire Department: 080

STAYING HEALTHY IN MALAGA

SUN AND WARMTH: Hydration is key: The sun's rays in Malaga can be intense, particularly in the summer. It's crucial to stay adequately hydrated by drinking plenty of water, aiming for at least two liters daily, regardless of thirst cues. | **OPT FOR SHADE:** Amidst the peak heat hours, typically from noon to 4 p.m., prioritize seeking shelter under shade or in air-conditioned spaces. Taking periodic breaks from exploration to unwind in a café or museum can offer respite. | **SHIELD YOURSELF FROM THE SUN**: Apply sunscreen with an SPF of 30 or higher generously, reapplying every two hours, especially after swimming or perspiring. Don't overlook safeguarding your lips and ears from sun exposure. Donning a wide-brimmed hat and sunglasses can provide further protection for your head and eyes. | **DIET AND HYDRATION:** Malaga boasts an array of locally sourced, fresh fruits, and vegetables. Seize the opportunity to incorporate these wholesome options into your meals and snacks. | **OPT FOR WHOLESOME FARE:** While the allure of local delicacies may be tempting, exercise mindfulness in your selections. Prioritize grilled or baked meats and fish, whole grains, and nourishing fats such as olive oil. | **LIMIT PROCESSED FOODS:** Processed snacks often harbor excessive sodium, sugar, and unhealthy fats. Curbing your consumption of these items can sustain your energy levels and promote overall well-being. | **CONSIDER WATER SOURCES:** While tap water is generally safe for consumption in Malaga, some individuals may prefer bottled water, especially if they have sensitive stomachs. | **STAY PHYSICALLY ACTIVE:** Engage in physical activities during your stay - strolling or cycling along the coastline, exploring the city on foot, or participating in a yoga session, staying active can invigorate your experience. | **PRIORITIZE ADEQUATE SLEEP:** Strive for 7-8 hours of nightly sleep to facilitate your body's rejuvenation and vitality.

18 ESSENTIAL APPS FOR VISITING MALAGA

If you are exploring Malaga for the first time, several apps can enhance your experience and help you navigate the city like a local. These apps include:

TOURISM APPS

1. WALKING AROUND MALAGA: This app let you discover Malaga at your own pace with guided walking tours led by local and international experts. This app is available offline for convenience. To download, go to: *http://tinyurl.com/MalagaVisitToursGuide* | **2. APP PICASSO MUSEUM MALAGA:** Immerse yourself in the world of Picasso with a comprehensive audio guide available in ten languages. Learn about his masterpieces and conveniently purchase museum tickets online. To download, go to: *http://tinyurl.com/MuseoPiccasoMalaga* | **3. APP MALAGA AUDIOGUIDES:** Gain insights into Malaga's main monuments & attractions with the official audio guide provided by the City Council. Access detailed information & plan your visits easily. To download, go to: *http://tinyurl.com/AudioTourOfficialMalaga*

URBAN TRANSPORT

4. APP METROPOLITAN TRANSPORT: Access essential information about public transportation services, including buses, the Metro de Malaga, and more, across various municipalities in the area including Malaga. To download, go to: *http://tinyurl.com/ConsorcioMalaga* | **5. INFOBUS MALAGA:** Get real-time information about bus arrivals, routes, and schedules for EMT buses in Malaga, ensuring smooth and efficient travel within the city. To download, go to: *http://tinyurl.com/InfoBusMalaga* | **6. METRO MALAGA:** Plan your metro journeys effortlessly with regular and special timetables, route maps, and top-up options for your travel card, all available through the official Metro Malaga app. To download, go to: *http://tinyurl.com/MetroMalaga* | **7. BICYCLE LANES MALAGA:** Discover bike lanes, parking spots, and navigate routes conveniently with this app designed for cyclists in and around Malaga. To download, go to: *http://tinyurl.com/BicycleLanesMalaga* | **8. BARRIOS MALAGA:** Uncover the unique character of Malaga's 400 neighborhoods, explore postal addresses, and locate yourself on the map with ease using this informative app. To download, go to: *http://tinyurl.com/BarriosMalagaApp*

9. UNIVERSITY OF MALAGA APP: Access comprehensive information about the University of Malaga, including academic programs, faculty details,

and campus locations. To download, go to: *http://tinyurl.com/UniOfMalaga*
| **10. THE MALAGA COSTA DEL SOL AIRPORT – FLIGHT TRACKER APP** furnishes comprehensive details about Malaga airport, along with real-time updates on arrivals and departures, complete with a flight tracker featuring maps. Additionally, it offers a world clock and currency converter for added convenience. To download, go to: *http://tinyurl.com/MalagaAirportInfo*

BEACHES

11. COSTASOLEANDO: The University of Malaga's app enables users to access information regarding the capacity of each beach, along with details such as temperature, wind conditions, wave heights, presence of seaweed, and potential sightings of jellyfish. To download, go to: *http://tinyurl.com/CostaSoleando* | **12. iPLAYA:** iPlaya offers information on over 2,000 beaches across the Spanish coastline, providing weather forecasts, water temperatures, swell conditions, tide schedules, UV indexes, and additional relevant details like sunrise and sunset times. Forecasts are sourced from the State Meteorological Agency. To download, go to: *http://tinyurl.com/iPlayaApp* | **13. MEDUSAPP**, specializing in jellyfish, addresses a common occurrence during the warmest months: the influx of jellyfish along the Costa del Sol coastline. This application enables users to verify the presence of jellyfish on beaches and provides alerts for sightings. To download, go to: *https://medusapp.net* | **14. INFOMEDUSA**, created by Aula del Mar, concentrates on the Malaga coast. It provides valuable insights into jellyfish species and offers guidance on treating stings. In addition to notifying users about sightings (allowing registered users to comment), the app furnishes further beach-related details such as temperature, wind conditions, sea state, solar radiation, and sky conditions. This application has been the author's go-to choice for years. To download, go to: *http://tinyurl.com/InfoMedusa* | **15. IMAR – SEA CONDITIONS:** iMar provides highly accurate details regarding sea conditions, allowing users to monitor parameters such as swell, wind speed and direction, atmospheric pressure, water temperature, and wave height with precision. To download, go to: *http://tinyurl.com/iMarSeaConditions* | **16. APP CHIRINGUÍA – BEACH BARS:** The Chiringuía app facilitates locating nearby beach bars, restaurants, and clubs, providing information on accessibility, proximity to the sand, parking availability, presence of amenities like sunbeds and restaurants, as well as features like chill-out areas. Users can also compile a list of favorite beach bars to stay updated on any developments. To download, go to: *http://tinyurl.com/Chiringuia* | **17. APP BLUE FLAGS:** The Blue Flags app serves as an indicator of the excellence of beaches and ports along the Malaga coastline, denoting a certification of quality. To download, go to: *http://tinyurl.com/AppBlueFlags* | **18. TODOSURF:** Surf's Up with Todosurf For surfing enthusiasts to stay updated on weather conditions, tides, and surfing forecasts worldwide, including insights specific to Malaga. To download, go to: *http://tinyurl.com/Todosurf*

TOURIST INFORMATION CENTERS

MUNICIPAL CENTRAL TOURIST OFFICE: Plaza de la Marina 11, 29001 Málaga | Tel: 951 926 020 | Opening Hours: 1st April to 31st October - Monday to Sunday: 9:00 to 20:00, 1st November to 31st March - Monday to Sunday: 9:00 to 18:00. Closed: 1st January and 25 December

BEN GABIROL VISITOR RECEPTION CENTER: Calle Granada 70, 29015 Málaga | Tel: 952 213 329

ALCAZABA INFORMATION POINT: Plaza Aduana, 29015 Málaga

AVENIDA DE ANDALUCIA INFORMATION POINT: Avenida Andalucia 1, 29002 Málaga

MALAGA AIRPORT: Avenida Comandante Garcia Morato 1, 29004 Málaga Terminal 3. Arrivals | Tel: 951 294 003 | Opening Hours: open every day, Monday - Friday 09:00 - 19:30, Saturday 09:30 - 19:30, Sundays and Holidays 09:30 - 15:00

TERMINAL PORTUARIA: Avenida Manuel Agustin Heredia 1, 29001 Málaga Estación marítima

CHINITAS PASSAGE: Pasaje de Chinitas , 4. | Tel: 951 308 911 | Opening Hours: Monday - Friday 09:00 - 19:30, Weekends and Holidays 09:30 - 15:00

TOURIST BOARDS: Provincial Malaga Tourism Agency: Turismo y Planificación Costa del Sol S.L.U. | Plaza de la Marina n4. Tel: +34 952 126 272 info@costadelsol.travel

CITY HALL OF MALAGA, TOURISM DEPARTMENT: Paseo Antonio Machado, 12, 5ª Planta, torre B - C.P. 29061 - MÁLAGA - Telf. 951 92 60 20 - info@malagaturismo.com

You can also find tourist information in one of the many kiosks which are scattered around Malaga City Centre, and the seafront.

SUSTAINABLE TRAVEL

Malaga stands out as a pioneer in sustainable tourism initiatives. Recognized for its commitment to promoting responsible travel, Malaga appeals to eco-conscious travelers seeking an environmentally friendly destination. Below are several ways to explore Malaga sustainably:

TRANSPORTATION: Opt for walking, cycling, or utilizing public transportation options such as buses, trams, and the metro, which are well-established in Malaga. Consider hybrid or electric taxis when necessary, or explore the city at your leisure by renting a bicycle from one of the many rental shops in the city center.

ACCOMMODATION: Choose accommodations committed to sustainability, looking for eco-certifications & practices such as energy-efficient appliances, water conservation, and recycling programs.

ACTIVITIES: Support local businesses and vendors to contribute to the local economy and sustainable practices. Visit the Malaga Farmers Market for fresh, locally sourced produce and explore the city's museums and historical sites on foot or by bike. Take day trips to nearby natural parks like Montes de Malaga or Sierra de las Nieves for outdoor activities such as hiking, biking, or birdwatching.

DINING: Opt for restaurants using local, seasonal ingredients to minimize the environmental impact of food transportation. Try vegetarian or vegan eateries to reduce your carbon footprint and support sustainable food practices. Be mindful of food waste and single-use items like plastic straws and cutlery.

Following these guidelines will not only reduce your environmental impact but also contribute to the local community, ensuring Malaga remains a vibrant and sustainable destination for generations to come.

7 WAYS TO MAKE YOUR MALAGAN TRIPS MORE ECO-FRIENDLY

1. EMBRACE LOCAL BUSINESSES: When in the Costa del Sol, opt for shopping at street markets and family-owned boutiques to support the local economy.

2. MINIMIZE TRANSFERS: Explore the diverse experiences within Malaga province without unnecessary transportation, aligning with sustainable travel principles.

3. PRIORITIZE ECO-CONSCIOUS CHOICES: Consider eco-friendly alternatives like biking instead of taxis, minimizing greenhouse gas emissions and reducing your carbon footprint.

4. RESPECT THE ENVIRONMENT: Leave natural areas untouched and clean by carrying extra bags for waste, recycling when possible, and refraining from taking anything from the environment.

5. AVOID POLLUTION: Opt for eco-friendly tourism activities such as cycling and quiet wildlife-friendly experiences, minimizing environmental impact.

6. ENGAGE IN LOW-IMPACT ACTIVITIES: Enjoy sports like golf or participate in eco-conscious events that reduce plastic usage and promote recycling.

7. EXPLORE CONVENTION TOURISM: Consider attending events in the Meetings, Incentives, Conferences, and Exhibitions (MICE) sector, which prioritize sustainability by limiting transfers and utilizing eco-friendly venues.

8. CONTRIBUTE TO THE COMMUNITY: Enhance your travel experience by volunteering in local community activities, aligning with the core values of sustainable travel.

55 USEFUL SPANISH LANGUAGE PHRASES

GREETINGS AND POLITENESS

- Hola! (***Oh-la!***) - Hello!
- Buenas! (**Bway-nas!**) - Hello! (Informal)
- Buenos días. (***Bway-nos dee-ahs***) - Good morning.
- Buenas tardes. (***Bway-nas tar-des***) - Good afternoon/evening.
- Buenas noches. (***Bway-nas no-ches***) - Good night.
- Gracias. (***Grah-see-ahs***) - Thank you.
- Muchas gracias. (***Moo-chas grah-see-ahs***) - Thank you very much.
- Por favor. (***Por fah-vor***) - Please.
- De nada. (***De nah-dah***) - You're welcome.
- Disculpe. (***Dis-kool-peh***) - Excuse me. (Formal)
- Disculpa. (***Dis-kool-pah***) - Excuse me. (Informal)
- Lo siento. (***Loh syen-toh***) - I'm sorry.

GETTING AROUND

- Dónde está...? (***Don-deh es-tah...***) - Where is...?
- Cómo puedo llegar a...? (***Coh-moh pweh-do yeh-gar ah...***) - How can I get to...?
- Cuánto cuesta...? (***Kwan-toh kweh-stah...***) - How much does it cost...?
- Un billete, por favor. (***Oon bee-yeh-teh, por fah-vor***) - One ticket, please.
- Parada. (***Pah-rah-dah***) - Stop.
- Taxi. (***Tahk-see***) - Taxi.

BASIC NEEDS

- Habla inglés? (***Ah-blah een-gles?***) - Do you speak English?
- No hablo español. (***Noh ah-bloh es-pan-yol***) - I don't speak Spanish.
- Me puede ayudar? (***Meh pweh-deh ah-yoo-dar?***) - Can you help me?
- Baño. (***Ban-yo***) - Bathroom.
- Agua. (*Ah-gwah*) - Water.
- Comida. (***Ko-mee-dah***) - Food.

USEFUL PHRASES

- Me gusta Málaga! (***Meh goos-tah Mah-lah-gah***!) - I like Malaga!
- Cuánto tiempo...? (***Kwan-toh tee-em-poh...***) - How long...?
- A qué hora...? (***Ah kay oh-rah...***) - At what time...?
- Salud! (***Sah-lood!***) - Cheers! (for toasts)

THE COMPLETE MALAGA TRAVEL GUIDE

- Que aproveche! (***Kay ah-pro-veh-che!***) - Enjoy your meal!

NUMBERS

- 1 - uno (oo-no) | ● 2 - dos (dohs) | ● 3 - tres (tres) | ● 4 - cuatro (kwah-tro) | ● 5 - cinco (seen-ko) | ● 6 - seis (sayes) | ● 7 - siete (sye-eh-teh) | ● 8 - ocho (oh-cho) | ● 9 - nueve (nway-veh) | ● 10 - diez (dyes)

SHOPPING

→ Cuánto cuesta esto? (***Kwan-toh kweh-stah es-to?***) - How much does this cost? | → Puedo ver...? (***Pweh-do ver...***) - Can I see...?
→ Tiene esto en...? (***Tyeh-neh es-to en...***) - Do you have this in...? (size, color)
→ Me lo llevo. (***Meh loh yeh-vo***) - I'll take it.

AT THE RESTAURANT

⇒ Hay una mesa para...? (***Igh ah una meh-sah pah-ra...***) - Is there a table for...? | ⇒ La carta, por favor. (***La kar-ta, por fah-vor***) - The menu, please. | ⇒ Me recomienda algo? (***Meh reh-koh-mee-en-da al-go?***) - Do you recommend anything?
⇒ Puede traerme la cuenta, por favor? (***Pweh-deh tray-eh-me la kwen-ta, por fah-vor?***) - Can I have the bill, please?

ASKING FOR DIRECTIONS

- Está lejos...? (***Es-tah leh-hos...***) - Is it far...?
- A la derecha o a la izquierda? (***Ah la deh-reh-cha o ah la ees-kyer-da?***) - Right or left?
- Puedo seguir recto? (***Pweh-do see-gweer reh-cto?***) - Can I continue straight? | ● Gracias por su ayuda! (***Grah-see-ahs por soo ah-yoo-dah!***) - Thank you for your help!

LEARNING ABOUT MALAGA

→ Qué se puede hacer aquí? (***Keh seh pweh-deh ah-ser ah-kee?***) - What can we do here? | → Cuál es la mejor época para visitar...? (***Kwal es la meh-hor eh-poh-kah pah-ra vee-see-tar...***) - What's the best time to visit...?
→ Me puedes contar un poco de la historia de...? (***Meh pweh-deh kon-tar oon poh-co de la ees-toh-ree-ah de...***) - Can you tell me a little about the history of...? | → Me encanta la cultura española! (***Meh en-kan-tah la kool-too-rah es-pan-yo-la!***) - I love Spanish culture!

BASIC VOCABULARY FOR MARKETS

- Qué es esto? = (**keh ehs ehs-toh?**) = What's that?
- Puedo probar? = (**pweh-doh proh-bahr?**) = Can I try?

187

- Qué rico! = (**keh ree-koh!**) = So tasty!
- Cómo se llama esto? = (**koh-moh seh yah-mah ehs-toh?**) = What's the name of that? | • Me da un kilo de x, por favor? = (**meh dah oon kee-loh deh (x), por fah-vor?**) = Can you give me one kilo of x, please? | • Cuánto cuesta? = (**kwan-toh kwehs-tah?**) = How much is it? | • Son productos locales? = (**sohn proh-dook-tohs loh-kah-les?**) = Are these local produce? | • Fresco (**fres-koh**) = Fresh
- Barato/ caro = (**bah-rah-toh / kah-roh**) = Cheap/ Expensive
- Cuarto y mitad = (**kwar-toh ee mee-tahd**) = 250g + 125g
- Mucha(s) gracia(s) = **moo-chah(s) grah-syah(s)** = Thank you very much (southern style) ;)

> Don't be afraid to make mistakes! Locals often appreciate the effort of visitors trying to speak their language, and they'll likely be happy to help you out.

MAP OF MALAGA WITH KEY POINTS OF INTEREST

SCAN THIS QR CODE TO EXPLORE THE MAP OF MALAGA WITH KEY POINTS OF INTEREST

3-DAY MALAGA ADENTURES ITINERARY

DAY 1: MORNING. Begin your day with a delightful breakfast at _La Cosmopolita_, a charming café nestled in the heart of Malaga. Next, embark on a guided exploration of the impressive _Alcazaba_ and _Roman Theatre_, delving into the city's rich historical tapestry. Then, take a leisurely stroll to the nearby _Malaga Cathedral_, an architectural gem that demands a visit.

AFTERNOON. For lunch, relish the authentic flavors of Andalusian cuisine at _El Meson de Cervantes_, renowned for its traditional culinary offerings. Following your meal, venture to the esteemed _Museo Picasso Málaga_, home to an extensive array of works by the iconic artist. Continue your cultural odyssey with a visit to the innovative _Centre Pompidou Málaga_, an art hub showcasing contemporary masterpieces.

EVENING. As dusk falls, treat yourself to a sumptuous dinner at _Restaurante José Carlos García_, a Michelin-starred culinary haven offering a gastronomic journey. Afterwards, immerse yourself in Malaga's lively nightlife scene with a visit to the _Malaga Pubs and Clubs Crawl_, where you can explore the city's finest bars and entertainment venues.

DAY 2: MORNING. Kickstart your day with a delectable breakfast at _La Reserva del Pastor Malaga Centro Historico_. Then, embark on an unforgettable journey to the awe-inspiring Caminito del Rey using the details provided in the Day trip to Caminito Del Rey section of this guide. Be captivated by the breathtaking landscapes and dramatic cliffs along this renowned pathway.

AFTERNOON. Following the exhilarating Caminito del Rey experience, indulge in a relaxed lunch at _La Deriva_, a charming eatery celebrated for its fresh seafood and locally sourced ingredients. Later in the afternoon, set off on a _Malaga Catamaran Sailing Trip with Sunset Option_, which cost just $12. (You can make a booking here: **http://tinyurl.com/MalagaCatamaranSailingTrip**) where you can unwind on the Mediterranean waters and admire the splendor of the sunset.

EVENING. Treat yourself to a memorable dinner at _Restaurante Skina_, a Michelin-starred culinary treasure renowned for its innovative cuisine. After dining, take a leisurely stroll along the picturesque _Malagueta Beach_ (Playa de La Malagueta) and bask in its tranquil ambiance.

DAY 3: MORNING. Commence your day with a delightful breakfast at *Tapeo de Cervantes*, a renowned establishment celebrated for its authentic Spanish culinary delights. Following breakfast, embark on a comprehensive full-day trip to the charming towns of Ronda and Setenil using the details provided in the day trip to Ronda section of this guide. Explore the breathtaking landscapes, visit iconic landmarks, and indulge in the local gastronomy.

AFTERNOON. Relish a leisurely lunch at *El Tintero II*, an exceptional seafood restaurant renowned for its unique dining experience where dishes are presented to your table on trays. Following your meal, take a leisurely stroll through the quaint streets of Ronda and Setenil, immersing yourself in the cultural richness and historical allure of these captivating locales.

EVENING. Conclude your Malaga escapade with a memorable dinner at *Refectorium Catedral*, an elegant restaurant renowned for its fusion of traditional and contemporary cuisine. Raise a glass to your unforgettable journey and reflect on the cherished memories created throughout your trip.

CONCLUSION

Using this Travel Guide as your indispensable companion, you will be able to embark on a journey to Malaga that transcends the ordinary and embraces the extraordinary. Malaga, a city brimming with history, culture, and endless opportunities for exploration, awaits your arrival with open arms. Let this travel guide be your steadfast companion as you navigate the sun-drenched streets, uncovering hidden gems tucked away in every corner. Immerse yourself in the vibrant tapestry of local flavors, indulging in culinary delights that tantalize the senses and ignite the soul.

But beyond the gastronomic delights and pristine beaches lies a city pulsating with life and adventure, beckoning you to delve deeper into its rich tapestry of experiences. Live like a local, embracing the rhythm of Malaga's heartbeat, and let the city unveil its secrets to you. As you bid farewell to this enchanting destination, carry with you not just memories, but a profound understanding of the magic that is Malaga—a place where every moment is an invitation to live life to the fullest.

BONUS: 43 EXCITING ACTIVITIES TO ENJOY IN MALAGA

Scan the QR Code below to request access to download the Bonus Attached to this Guide Titled: **43 Fun Things To Do in Malaga**

OTHER BOOKS BY THIS AUTHOR

OSLO TRAVEL GUIDE: Your Essential Travel Companion to Explore Norway's Vibrant Capital - Top Must-See Attractions, History, Culture, Adventure And Unique Experiences.

NEW ZEALAND TRAVEL GUIDE 2024: Your Essential Companion for An Ultimate Experience in the Land of the Long White Cloud

TRAVEL GUIDE 2024: Discover the Best Sights, Activities, & Restaurants to Experience Umbria's Rich Food, Wine, Culture, & Natural Wonders within its Rolling Countryside

PUGLIA TRAVEL GUIDE: Your Ultimate Companion to Italy's Enchanting South – Unveiling Secret Spots, Timeless Traditions, and Breathtaking Landscapes for an Experience of a Lifetime

NAPLES AND THE AMALFI COAST TRAVEL BOOK: A Simplified Guide To Plan And Explore Naples & Amalfi Coast including information on Where to stay, Things To Try Out & Itineraries

Scan the QR Code Above or Click the Link below to See More books from this Author (All Books are Available in Kindle, Paperback and Hardcover)

CLICK HERE TO SEE ALL BOOKS BY THIS AUTHOR

ABOUT THE AUTHOR

Nicholas Ingram is a seasoned travel enthusiast and a passionate writer with a deep love for exploring new places and immersing in diverse cultures. With a wealth of experience spanning over 23 years, Nick has become a trusted voice in the world of travel writing.

Nick embarked on his first solo adventure at the age of 21, and since then he hasn't looked back. Nick believes that travel is not just about visiting new destinations, but about forging connections with people, understanding their way of life, and embracing the beauty of our world.

As a seasoned travel guide writer, Nick has authored more than 10 books and numerous articles on destinations around the globe. Nick is known for his ability to provide readers with comprehensive, practical, and inspiring insights into the places he cover. Nick doesn't just stop at guidebooks. He is a firm believer in sustainable travel and actively advocate for responsible tourism. His writings often emphasize the importance of respecting local communities and preserving the natural environment. When Nick isn't busy penning down travel guides, you can find him seeking out hidden gems, indulging in local cuisines, or engaging in meaningful conversations with fellow travelers. His curiosity knows no bounds, and he is always on the lookout for the next great adventure.

WEBSITE: https://www.amazon.com/stores/author/B0C2LVJY5W/about | https://www.amazon.com/author/nicholasingram | https://www.amazon.com/stores/author/B0C2LVJY5W/allbooks | **EMAIL:** *theworldexplorergs@gmail.com* | **X (FORMERLY TWITTER):** *@daworldexplorer*

Printed in Great Britain
by Amazon